Hear the Lion Roar

SHERRI WILSON

Copyright © 2013 Sherri Wilson

All rights reserved.

ISBN: 0615817203
ISBN-13: 978-0615817200

DEDICATION

To my husband for always believing in me, supporting, and encouraging me to pursue the Lord's will no matter what it is.

CONTENTS

1	The Revelation	1
2	Ephesus	5
3	Smyrna	21
4	Pergamos	39
5	Thyatira	61
6	Sardis	78
7	Philadelphia	97
8	Laodicea	117
	Bibliography	137

1 THE REVELATION

I, John, both your brother and companion in the tribulation and kingdom and patience of Jesus Christ was on the island that is called Patmos for the word of God and for the testimony of Jesus Christ. I was in the Spirit on the Lord's Day, and I heard behind me a loud voice, as of a trumpet, saying, "I am the Alpha and Omega, the First and the Last," and, "What you see, write in a book and send it to the seven churches which are in Asia: to Ephesus, to Smyrna, to Pergamos, to Thyatira, to Sardis, to Philadelphia, and to Laodicea" (Revelation 1:9-11).

One day in prayer, Holy Spirit said, "If you look up the meaning of the names of each church in Revelation, you will find that the meaning of their names relates to their condition at the time and the message I gave each of them." The Holy Spirit knew my curious nature would require investigation. I looked up the name for each church and compared its meaning to the message given, and I was amazed to find that each name perfectly corresponded to the message the Lord gave each church. My curiosity was even more piqued. I then wanted to know the history of each city. Does it exist today? What was its culture like? Was the city kind or unkind to the new Christian sect? I also wanted to discover the meaning of some of the promises given to each church that were veiled in seemingly cryptic phrases. What does it mean to be a pillar in the temple of God? What is the significance of receiving a white stone?

As I studied, I realized that the messages to these churches weren't just for them, but they are for us today. God began to show me that many local churches, denominations, and Christians as a whole in all countries fell under one or more of the churches in Revelation. I knew that the Spirit wanted to speak His ancient message again for our generation.

However, I was intimidated at first. The book of Revelation is one of the most difficult books to understand, yet it also holds the most awesome blessing to those who read it (Revelation 1:3). God immediately taught me that Revelation is not a revelation of the beast and his false prophet or of the enemy's end-time plans. According to Revelation 1:1, it is a revelation of Jesus Christ. In order to properly interpret Revelation, one must keep Jesus as the center. If He is not the center, the result is an out of balance end-time doctrine; therefore, I knew to be aware of any pet doctrines or ideas that could eclipse Christ as the center as I studied His messages to the seven churches.

The Greek word for "revelation" is *apokalupsis*, which means disclosure, manifestation, appearing, coming, lighten, be revealed.[1] Basically, God took the lid off and disclosed to John what the last of the last days would be like. When studying Revelation, it is extremely important to keep one's spiritual eyes focused on Christ or the reader will begin to fear the things written in Revelation. Satan knows that scripture says that anything not of faith is sin (Rom. 14:23). Fear is the opposite of faith and will produce deception.

You might be wondering if it is necessary to understand Revelation. Who can possibly understand it anyway? If I live right and in God's will, won't I be okay regardless of when and how these things take place? I've heard some say that they aren't pre-tribulation or post-tribulation believers but that they are pan-tribulation believing that everything will "pan" out in the end. If God didn't feel it necessary for us to understand the end of this age, why did He devote an entire book to this very subject not to mention the hundreds, if not thousands, of prophecies devoted to the last days? I will say prophetically that I believe as we near the end of this age, greater revelation will be released concerning the book of Revelation. Anyone who is intimate with the Lord will desire to know His plan for the end of the age because that is on His heart as well as the final uniting of the Bridegroom with His bride forever. The end is in actuality the beginning. The Spirit shares what He hears including things to come (Jn. 16:13), and may we hear what He is saying to this generation.

Revelation was given to the apostle John who was quite old when he was exiled to an island because of his faith and bold testimony of Christ during intense persecution at the hands of the Roman emperor Nero. John called himself a brother and companion in the tribulation that Christians were under during Nero's reign. "Tribulation" in Revelation 1:9 means pressure. Jesus correlated tribulation with birth pangs by using the word "sorrows" in Matthew 24:8. "Sorrows" means a pang especially in childbirth.[2] What is interesting is that the island John was on was called Patmos, which means my killing. Often God uses tribulation or pressures to purify us or to *kill* the fleshly nature in us before He *births* His purposes in our lives. It is significant that He chose to reveal Jesus Christ's revelation to John while he was in exile due to tribulation on an island whose name means "my killing." The amount of flesh nature we allow God to crucify is the degree to which we see Jesus manifested in our lives for only then can His nature be birthed in us.

Jesus called Himself "the Alpha and Omega, the First and the Last." Alpha is the first letter of the Greek alphabet, and Omega is the last letter of the Greek alphabet. Jesus was saying, "I am the beginning of all things, and I am the end of all things." Practically this means that everything that you are going through now and will go through in the future, whether from God, the result of sin, or the result of others' actions, will be used by the Lord to transform us into His image.

> And we know that all things work together for good to
> those who love God, to those who are called according
> to His purpose. For whom He foreknew, He also
> predestined to be conformed to the image of His son,
> that He might be the firstborn among many brethren
> (Rom. 8:28, 29).

Setting the stage with these words, He then instructed John to deliver a message to seven churches that were in Asia: Ephesus, Smyrna, Pergamos, Thyatira, Sardis, Philadelphia, and Laodicea. John turned to see who was speaking to him and saw seven golden lampstands and in the midst a Man clothed with a garment down to His feet and girded about the chest with a golden band. His head and hair were white as snow and His eyes were a flame of fire. His feet were like refined brass and His voice the sound of many waters. In His right hand He held seven stars and out of His mouth came a two-edged sword. His countenance was like the sun shining in its strength. When John saw Him, he fell at His feet as if dead (Rev. 1:12-17). Remember, John had laid his head on

Jesus' breast (John 13:25), was the disciple whom Jesus loved (John 13:23, 20:2), and took care of His mother after His crucifixion (John 19:25-27), but when he saw the resurrected King, John fell on his face in terror.

After Jesus reassured John, He again instructed him to write down the things he saw, and He explained the mystery of the seven stars in His hand and the seven golden lampstands.

> The mystery of the seven stars which you saw in My right hand, and the seven golden lampstands: The seven stars are the angels of the seven churches, and the seven lampstands which you saw are the seven churches (Revelation 1:20).

The word "angel" is the Greek word *aggelos* and means messenger and by implication can mean pastor.[3] Before Jesus gave His message for each church, He would direct John to write to the "angel of the church." More than likely He meant the pastor or shepherd of that church.

The use of seven is also significant. Seven is a cardinal (supreme) number that denotes sufficiency.[4] It comes from the Hebrew word *saba,* which means to sate or to fill to satisfaction.[5] It was often translated filled, enough, and satisfied. Seven is symbolic of completeness or perfection. That He gave seven messages to seven churches means that He gave a complete message to the complete church--past, present, and future.

Before we begin our study of the first church, Ephesus, I want to awe you with God's sovereignty. The seven churches were located in cities in Asia Minor, which is modern-day Turkey. Each city was located at the base of the Taurus Mountains. In the heavens is a constellation called Taurus, which is a bull. Within Taurus is a cluster of stars known as the Pleiades's. Pleiades's consists of a main star that is surrounded by seven other stars. I'm sure you can see the parallel. Jesus is the main star and the seven stars are the angels of the seven churches (Rev. 1:20). What is even more interesting is that Pleiades's means "congregation of the ruler," and in Arabic it means "center." Both ancient Arabs and Jews considered the Pleiades's the center of the universe.[6] Remember to keep Jesus the center.

> The heavens declare the glory of God; and the firmament shows His handiwork (Ps. 19:1).

2 EPHESUS

To the angel of the church of Ephesus write...
(Revelation 2:1)

Ephesus was the most important commercial city in Asia Minor. It is here that the temple of Diana, also known as Artemis, was built. It took 220 years to build and was one of the seven wonders of the Ancient World. In the center of the temple court was an image of the goddess Diana, which people believed fell from heaven (Acts 19:35).

Ephesus had a theater that could hold 50,000 spectators, which was the largest structure of its kind and a stadium that held foot races, wrestling matches, and fights with wild beasts. Some of the games were held in honor of Diana for she was the most important deity in Ephesus. Her importance wasn't just spiritual but was also commercially motivated. She brought much prosperity to merchants who made her image, to those who sponsored the games, and to the priests who received the offerings to her temple as evidenced by the riot that took place during Paul's stay when this prosperity was threatened (Acts 19:21-41). The church of Ephesus was located here in this wealthy idol-infested city.

GREETING

> These things says He who holds the seven stars in His right hand, who walks in the midst of the seven golden lampstands (Revelation 2:1).

Remember that the stars are the messengers of the churches (Revelation 1:20). Jesus holds these stars in His right hand, which signifies power and authority. "Holds" is the Greek word *krateo*[1] and means literally "to use strength, that is, to seize or retain." According to *Thayer's Greek Definitions*, it means to have power, to be chief, to be master, to take possession of, and to hold in the hand.[2] Jesus was declaring His power, authority, strength and possession of the seven stars or pastors. "Walks" means to tread all around, that is, walk at large (especially as proof of ability) and is also a present active participle, which means it is a continuous action.[3] Remember that the lampstands are the churches and that seven means complete or full. Today, Jesus Christ as Supreme Master full of all power continuously walks in the midst of the entire body of Christ. As King, He exercises His power, authority, and strength as needed in His kingdom and in His church.

EXORTATION

> I know your works, your labor, your patience, and that you cannot bear those who are evil. And you have tested those who say they are apostles and are not, and have found them liars, and you have persevered and have patience, and have labored for My name's sake and have not become weary (Revelation 2:2,3).

Jesus commended the church at Ephesus for its works, labor, and patience. Obviously, Ephesus was a church with a purpose, which suits the meaning of its name—fully purposed. Jesus also commended them for not bearing or enduring those who were evil, which implies that they kept themselves separate amidst the idolatry that was prevalent in their society. Jesus also commended them for testing those who claimed to be apostles but were not. Sadly, this is something the modern church has lost.

Testing Apostles

The word "apostle" means he that is sent.[4] In the last decade, God has begun to restore the apostolic office. Even so, the enemy always sends his "apostles" first to pervert the office and cause God's people to reject all apostles because of the abuse of other so-called apostles. Today, we have many who are called apostles and many who claim to be apostles, yet the church is not testing them. As a matter of fact, our first indication that a person is not an apostle is if the person goes around saying he is an apostle to everyone who will listen. A person cannot send himself as an apostle to the Body of Christ no matter how much he asserts his "apostolic position." Remember that apostle means "he that is sent" not "he that sends himself." It is for the body to judge whether a person is an apostle or not (1 Cor. 11:15; Rev. 2:2; 1 Jn. 4:1-3). For that matter, it is for us to judge whether a person is a prophet, evangelist, teacher, or pastor. One who has a true calling will not need to proclaim who he is unless he is defending his God-given position. Paul often had to defend his position as an apostle against those who tried to undermine his authority.

"Apostle" also means ambassador.[5] Ambassadors were chosen from a select group of mature, experienced men of the royal court sent to a foreign country to represent the king and his interests. He was intimate with the king of his country and knew his mind on political matters. An ambassador usually stayed in a country for only two years so he didn't become too sympathetic to the foreign country and betray his king. To a degree, we are all called as apostles because we are sent to a dying world to represent Christ carefully and effectively.

What are some characteristics of apostles? First, apostles are mature Christians knowledgeable in the Word and in His ways. Second, apostles are spiritual fathers (1 Cor. 4:15,16, Gal. 4:19). Third, apostles are often commissioned by a physical appearance of Christ so that he or she is a witness of the resurrected Christ (Luke 6:12-16, Acts 1:22; 9:1-19). Fifth, apostles are fiercely devoted to spreading the gospel even enduring intense persecution and physical discomfort to do so (1 Cor. 6:4-10). And, finally, signs, wonders, and mighty deeds follow apostles. Most are awed by the title of apostle and by the mighty works. However, signs and wonders can be deceptive (Deut. 13:1-3, 2; Thess. 2:9). You must examine the fruit (Mt. 7:20).

False Apostles

> For such are false apostles, deceitful workers, transforming themselves into apostles of Christ. And no wonder! For Satan himself transforms himself into an angel of light. Therefore it is no great thing if his ministers also transform themselves into ministers of righteousness, whose end will be according to their works (2 Cor. 11:13-15).

For years, I missed the fact that the context of these verses was Paul defending his authority as an apostle against false apostles who were criticizing him. These false apostles were seeking to lead astray Paul's flock for selfish motives. They appeared to be apostles but their hearts were unchanged. That is why Paul said that these "false apostles" were "deceitful workers" who transformed themselves into "apostles of Christ," which shouldn't amaze us because the Evil One himself transforms himself into an angel of light. His ministers even appear to be "ministers of *righteousness*."

One day I decided to study the word "transforms" in verse 14 to gain a better understanding of how such men can convince so many. "Transforms" is *metaschematizo* in the Greek and means to transfigure or disguise.[6] Transfigure caught my attention, and I thought of Jesus being transfigured on the mount. I looked that word up also. To my surprise, "transfigure" is a similar Greek word, *metamorphoo*.[7] I dug deeper and discovered something very interesting. In Zodhiates' *The Complete Word Study Dictionary: New Testament*, *metaschematizo* was compared against *metamorphoo*. *Metaschematizo* is only an outward change of form, but *metamorphoo* is an internal transformation that changes the very essence of someone or something. The example given was of two gardens. If you have a Japanese garden that you change into an Italian garden, it is still a garden, which is *metaschematizo*. However, if you take that garden and change it into a ballpark, it is *metamorphoo*. The essence of the garden was changed until it was no longer a garden.[8] In Christians, *metamorphoo* is a change from the inside out, which is a work that only the Holy Spirit can do. The false apostles Paul was speaking of had not had a genuine change of their hearts or essence.

There are two scriptures that use *metamorphoo* in the context of change that will help us understand exactly what God wants to do in us. In these scriptures, *metamorphoo* is translated transformed.

> And do not be conformed to this world, but be **transformed** by the renewing of your mind, that you may prove what is that good and acceptable and perfect will of God (Rom. 12:2).

> But we all with unveiled face, beholding as in a mirror the glory of the Lord, are being **transformed** into that same image from glory to glory, just as by the Spirit of the Lord (2 Cor. 3:18).

Jesus told us that a tree is known by its fruit. A bad tree cannot produce good fruit and vice versa (Matt. 7:16-18). Fruit trees also produce fruit of their own kind. An apple tree will not bear oranges. A pear tree will not bear peaches. A person who is not being changed from the inside out cannot bear good fruit. Of course, this changing is a process. Anyone recently saved will not have much fruit at all. But apostles should have bushels of fruit. Study the fruit of the Spirit in Galatians 5:22, 23 so you may recognize God's fruit in yourself and others.

In discerning false apostles, it is often not feasible to examine all their fruit at one church service. You must know a person to do this. However, any pastor that allows anyone to minister to his flock should have already investigated that person's fruit. I know of one pastor who called a minister's neighbors and asked them to describe him as a neighbor. Was he kind? How did he treat them? Was his speech and lifestyle godly? He learned that this minister did not live like he preached so he refused to allow him to minister to his flock.

Even if we can't go to those lengths, we do have the discernment of the Spirit. We need to listen to what He is saying to us concerning any minister, but remember that discernment is based in love (Eph. 1:9). If you harbor offense and unforgiveness, your discernment will be clouded. Also, the gift of discernment isn't solely for discerning demons and evil, but it is for discerning the Spirit's work and Christ in other people and ministries. Also, examine the fruit produced by a minister during his services. Do you leave the meeting with peace? Are you encouraged to come up higher in your walk? Or do you leave feeling condemned, manipulated, and beaten? Also remember that anything taught must line up with the Word, which requires that you have regular study times so you can recognize the false from the real. For example, I'm not a diamond expert. If someone tried to sell me cubic zirconium as diamonds, I would not know how to tell the difference. If I purchased the "diamonds" anyway, it would be my fault for wasting my money. Ignorance is not an excuse for being deceived.

One morning the pastor of a church I went to announced a guest speaker was coming to minister. The pastor called him an apostle. I immediately pictured in my mind the great apostles of the New Testament—Peter, John, and Paul. I was excited and decided to go to the meetings. The first night of meetings was great. The teaching was good, and I felt an anointing. At the time I ignored certain things such as the speaker throwing in little tidbits of information that was not supported by the Word and an anointing that began to feel oppressive instead of peaceful. After two nights of teaching, I decided that my in-laws needed to come hear this "apostle."

The atmosphere of the last night was completely different. I felt uncomfortable and restless. I did not feel the Holy Spirit at all. The congregation seemed tense and on edge. The first part of the meeting began much the same as the other two nights, but after about 20 minutes of teaching, the speaker switched gears so smoothly I didn't notice at first. Suddenly, he began to flatter the pastor by telling him grandiose visions he had received from God of the pastor preaching to foreign nations with thousands upon thousands in attendance. Even though the pastor was visibly uncomfortable, he didn't say anything.

Next, the speaker began to berate the congregation for being stingy and selfish by not giving more money to the church. He even threatened to send down God's judgment upon them if they didn't give more. At this point I wondered what was happening. This gifted speaker had suddenly turned into a raving lunatic! After this beating of words, the speaker then used manipulation and hype to get people to give. Guilt made its way around the church condemning everyone for not giving more. I even felt its effects as I had not yet learned that the Holy Spirit doesn't motivate us to give by guilt (Rom. 8:1) If guilt didn't work, hype finished the job by promising financial breakthroughs and material blessings for those who gave. I was confused and stunned.

After the meeting, I followed my in-laws home to discuss what had happened. We immediately recognized that different spirits other than the Holy Spirit were at work. We didn't condemn the speaker, but we did get out our Bibles and tested to see if he was an apostle or not. The Holy Spirit showed us scripture after scripture proving that he was not. He showed us the different demonic spirits that were at work in the meeting including familiar spirits that produced a false anointing, and He pointed out that there were no signs and wonders and mighty deeds. He then showed us the doctrine that was preached was not based on the Word. Even though we were saddened that many did not see what had happened, we were also elated that God revealed to us that this man was not an apostle. We knew it was by the grace of God not our own discernment.

Christians tend to be too accepting of others, which could be due in part to the scripture that love believes all things (1 Cor. 13:7). However, Jesus warned us repeatedly about wolves in sheep's clothing and not to be deceived. The apostle John told us not to believe every spirit but test them to see whether they are of God (1 John 4:1-6). It is a balance. Yes, we are not to be suspicious, but we are not to entrust ourselves to everyone (John 2:24,25). We are to search the scriptures **daily** to see whether any teaching we hear or read is true (Acts 17:11, 2 Tim. 2:15). We should study on our own so that when we hear a teaching that does not sound right, we have enough Word in us to discern its truth or lack of truth even more so in these latter days. The epistles are full of admonitions about false teachers and false prophets that will help to carry some Christians away from the faith, which is the fulfillment of 2 Thess. 2:3:

> Let no one deceive you by any means; for that Day will not come unless the falling away comes first, and the man of sin is revealed, the son of perdition.

We must have a love for the truth, and according to Jesus, He is the Truth (John 14:6).

> The coming of the lawless one is according to the working of Satan, with all power, signs, and lying wonders, and with all unrighteous deception among those who perish, **because they did not receive the love of the truth**, that they might be saved (2 Thess. 2:9,10).

> If there arises among you a prophet or a dreamer of dreams, **and he gives you a sign or wonder, and the sign or wonder comes to pass**, of which he spoke to you, saying, "Let us go after others gods"--which you have not known--"and let us serve them," you shall not listen to the words of that prophet or that dreamer of dreams, **for the Lord your God is testing you to know whether you love the Lord your God with all your heart and with all your soul** (Deut. 13:1-3).

Do not allow signs and wonders to deceive you. We must remember that Satan's apostles come as ministers of righteousness. Judas Iscariot was part of the Twelve, the men closest to Christ, yet he betrayed Jesus and is the only other person in the Word other than the antichrist that is called "the son of perdition" and this from Jesus' own mouth (Jn 17:12)! We are to be wise as serpents and harmless (innocent) as doves (Matt. 10:16). Beware of seeking after miracles, signs, and wonders. These have their place, but they must not become our center.

An Enduring Church

> I know you are enduring patiently and are bearing up for My name's sake, and you have not fainted or become exhausted or grown weary (Rev. 2:3 AMP).

Enduring patiently. Bearing up. Fainted. Exhausted. Weary. These words tell us that the church at Ephesus didn't have it easy. The word "patience" in verse 3 means to endure things or circumstances especially trial and suffering in faith and duty. It also means to persevere and to remain under.[9] Patience is only gained by trial (Rom. 5:3, James

1:3). For some of us, a trial is waiting in line at a grocery store or getting stuck driving behind a slow poke. And if we take advantage of these opportunities, patience will develop. But the church at Ephesus wasn't enduring long lines and slow drivers. Instead, the Christians at Ephesus had to defend their faith against various onslaughts of false doctrine, false apostles, and unbelievers that felt they betrayed their gods by worshiping Christ. And in doing so it cost some of them their income, homes, comfort, security, and even their lives. The Ephesian church seemed to have it together--labored for Christ without growing weary, tested false apostles, and even endured persecution. But a crucial element was missing.

> Nevertheless I have this against you, that you have left your first love (Rev. 2:4).

I believe one of the greatest temptations to ministers is the belief that ministry replaces intimacy with Christ. I have been tempted many times to think that because I wrote a teaching one day or I ministered to someone another day that I have spent my "time" with the Lord. Yet He has repeatedly reminded me that ministry is not the same as spending quality intimate time with Him. It is similar to a man and woman falling in love. At first, there is the initial attraction, but the more time they spend together, the more their love for each other grows. That love is finally expressed in its fullest in the marriage bed where they become one. As we spend time in His presence, we get to know Him better and our love for Him increases.

> I do not pray for these alone, but also for those who will believe in Me through their word; that they all may be one, as You, Father, are in Me, and I in You; that they also may be one in Us, that the world may believe that You sent Me. And the glory which You gave Me I have given them, that they may be one just as We are one: I in them, and You in Me; that they may be made perfect in one, and that the world may know that You have sent Me, and have loved them as You have loved Me. Father, I desire that they also whom You gave Me may be with Me where I am, that they may behold My glory which

> You have given Me; for You loved Me before the
> foundation of the world. O righteous Father! The world
> has not known You, but I have known You; and these
> have known that You sent Me. And I have declared to
> them Your name, and will declare it, that the love with
> which You loved Me may be in them, and I in them
> (John 17:20-26).

One of Jesus' prayers right before His arrest was for those who believe in Him after He is gone, which includes us. He asked the Father that we may all be one and that we may be in Him and He in us. He also asked that the love the Father has for His Son would be in us. It is only when we have the Father's love in us can we love others. He grows this love slowly by showing us how much He truly loves us. After we firmly grasp God's love for us, we are then able to love others, which increases unity in the church.

> And this is eternal life, that they may know You, the
> only true God, and Jesus Christ whom You have sent
> (John 17:3).

Eternal life is knowing the Father and the Son. The word "know" in this verse is the same know used in Luke 1:34 when Mary asked the angel how she could become pregnant without first knowing a man. It is a word that suggests sexual intimacy between a married man and woman. It also suggests spiritual intimacy between an individual and God. Jesus told Nicodemus that he had to be born again to *see* the kingdom of God, but to *enter* he had to be born of water and the Spirit (John 3:3,5). It is the Spirit that leads us into intimacy with God.

> But we all, with unveiled face, beholding as in a mirror
> the glory of the Lord, are being transformed into the
> same image from glory to glory, just as **by the Spirit of
> the Lord** (2 Cor. 3:18).

You see, it is not the works or ministry that we do that guarantees our entrance into His kingdom. The Ephesians were busy with ministry and much more, but they had left their first love. "Left" in Revelation 2:4 means to send forth or away, to let go from oneself, and in this case to leave, desert, or quit.[10] It was probably a slow process. First, the demands of church slowly began to take precedence. When the Spirit tugged at their hearts for them to escape into His arms for a bit, they probably shrugged Him off and continued with "the work of the Lord." After a while, they no longer sensed His urgings because their conscience was seared. They lacked love for the One they were zealous for.

> Not everyone who says to Me, "Lord, Lord," shall enter the kingdom of heaven, but he who does the will of My Father in heaven. Many will say to Me in that day, "Lord, Lord, have we not prophesied in Your name, cast out demons in Your name, and done many wonders in Your name?" And then I will declare to them, "I never **knew** you; depart from Me, you who practice lawlessness!" (Matt. 7:21-23)

"Knew" in Matthew 7:23 is the same Greek word mentioned earlier for sexual intimacy. God desperately longs for those who are head-over-heals in love with Him. He isn't interested in Christians who only "date" Him. He wants long-term commitment in covenant relationship. Out of that intimacy should flow miracles and wonders. Does this mean that you can't minister until you are strongly in love with Him? No, the apostles ministered along side Jesus, and they hadn't yet reached that level of love that He desired. But the Bible promises that the Holy Spirit pours out His love into our hearts (Rom. 5:5). I believe it is in seed form and grows as we water it with His presence.

When we stop spending time with Him, we are no longer being transformed into His image, which will lead to sin. Notice that Jesus told those to depart from Him that *practiced* lawlessness. First John 3:4 says that sin is lawlessness. Lawlessness is basically disobedience. This type of lawlessness does not describe a Christian who struggles with certain areas of sin but is working with God for change. The phrase--practice makes perfect--comes to mind. These have made a habit of willfully and knowingly disobeying the Lord's voice and Word. These still minister in His name, but their eternal lives are in danger.

God taught me about the importance of "looking" like His Son through my relationship with my sister. We were separated when I was four, and she was an infant. We were later reconciled when I was 16, and she was 12. Even though we didn't know each other and had been separated for 14 years, we had many of the same expressions, mannerisms, and speech patterns. Why? We were family. When we stand before the Father, He will be looking for one thing--His Son's image whether in infant or mature form. We must remember that we will be transformed into what we behold for good or bad (2 Cor. 3:17-18).

Repent

> Remember therefore from where you have fallen; repent and do the first works, or else I will come to you quickly and remove your lampstand from its place--unless you repent (Rev.2:5).

"Remember" means to call to mind.[11] The Amplified Bible says to "remember from the heights you've fallen." God's throne is on a mount. When we enter His presence, we are entering His throne room on that mount. He was telling the Ephesians to think back, to remember when they stopped doing the first works of intimacy with Him. Was it disobedience? Was it busyness? Was it pride or unforgiveness? Was it ignoring the Spirit's promptings for intimacy? Was it spiritual laziness?

The word "fallen" in verse 5 means to fall from any state or condition.[12] "Repent" denotes a change of place or condition, and it also means to restore to right condition.[13] It is similar to a man and his friend walking on a path conversing intimately. They both come to a fork in the road, and the man takes the fork and the friend continues down the same path. At first the man doesn't notice any change in their intimacy because his new path isn't too far away from his friend's path, but after a time he senses a distance between him and his friend. His friend tries to tell him the problem, but the man is too busy talking and walking. Finally, he can't hear his friend's voice and he stops. He looks around and notices that he is alone. He has two choices: he can either find his way back or be mad at his friend for deserting him. If he decides to find his way back, he must first remember where he strayed (at the fork), repent (or turn around), and meet up with his friend who is waiting for him (restoration).

John the Baptist said to "bear fruits worthy of repentance" (Luke 3:8). Repentance is not asking forgiveness and then continuing down the same path. Repentance is taking active, practical steps to restoration. With the Holy Spirit's leading, you can have the intimate relationship with Him that He desires and demands. However, Jesus warned the Ephesians what would happen if they didn't repent--"I will come to you quickly and remove your lampstand from its place."

Lampstand is a symbol of the church (Rev. 1:20). The lampstand was an article of the tabernacle and later the temple that was located in the Holy Place across from the table of showbread with the altar of incense between them. The lampstand was filled with pure oil pressed from olives and provided the only light in the Holy Place representing the anointing of the Holy Spirit. It was the job of the priests to tend to the lampstand from evening to morning. Today, the church is to carry the anointing of the Holy Spirit and be a light in a dark place. We, too, are to tend carefully to our relationship with God so that our light continues to shine.

The word "anointing" is *chrisma*, and it means to smear and figuratively the endowment of the Holy Spirit. It comes from a word that means to smear or rub with oil and by implication to consecrate to an office or religious service.[14] It is akin to *charomai*, which means to furnish what is needed.[15] If it wasn't for the lampstand in the Holy Place, there would be no light for the priests to tend to the table of showbread or the altar of incense. Jesus was telling the Ephesians that if they didn't repent, He would quickly come and remove the anointing He had placed upon them. A lack of love and intimacy with Him will extinguish our light and the anointing will be removed.

This is what happened to Eli the High Priest of the city of Shiloh. He refused to discipline his sons, which resulted in judgment of his family line. I also believe he was no longer intimate with God because there was no widespread revelation when he was high priest (1 Sam. 3:1). Revelation is simply a byproduct of spending time with the God. He shares things with His friends (Jn. 15:15; Gen. 18:17). Because of Eli's disobedience, the Philistines stole the ark. When Eli heard, he fell over backward off a bench and died. The ark represented the abiding presence of God. God removed His presence, and it never returned to Shiloh. Shiloh ceased to be the location where God dwelt because it no longer had what was needed.

THE PROMISE

After Jesus concluded His exhortation, He then promised the Ephesian Christians something wonderful if they repented and overcame:

> He who has an ear, let him hear what the Spirit says to the churches. To him who overcomes I will give to eat from the tree of life, which is in the midst of the Paradise of God (Rev. 2:7).

This promise is a profound promise with a long history. In the beginning, God created the earth and then man. After He created man, God planted a garden and placed the man there to tend to it (Gen. 2:8). God put two trees in this garden that would determine the future of mankind—the tree of life and the tree of the knowledge of good and evil (Gen. 2:9). He then told Adam that he could eat of every tree but the tree of the knowledge of good and evil. Many question why God did this, but without the chance of disobedience, there is no true obedience. The Garden of Eden and the tree of life were physical representations of the heavenly garden and tree of life (Heb. 9:23-24; Rev. 22:2). Both of these trees were in the midst of the Garden of Eden.

We all know that Adam failed in this test, which caused a separation in his relationship with God. In order to protect mankind, God sent Adam and Eve out of the garden and away from the tree of life. God knew that if Adam or Eve ate from that tree, mankind would forever be doomed to a fallen state. He then placed angels east of the garden to guard the *way* to the tree of life (Gen. 3:22-24). Thousands of years later, He sent Jesus.

Jesus stated, "I am the *Way,* the Truth, and the Life" (Jn. 14:6). By His sacrifice on the cross, Jesus opened the way to the tree of life again, which is located in the Paradise of God in heaven (2 Cor. 12:4). "Paradise" is a Persian word that means garden specifically Eden.[16] Adam failed to guard the intimacy he had with the Father, and the

Ephesian Christians were also failing this test. All of us must guard our relationship with God because it will result in eternal life or forever eating from the tree of life. Notice the tree of life was in the center of the garden, which prophetically tells us that Jesus is to be the center of our lives. Any time He isn't, it results in us eating from the wrong tree.

APPLICATION

The promise to the Ephesian Christians is for all of us. Notice that the Bible says, "...to *he* who has an ear to hear" not "...to the *church* who has an ear to hear." This makes it each individual's responsibility to overcome. We cannot blame others or our churches for our irresponsibility. The blaming game has been around since the beginning (Gen. 3:12-13), but God puts is squarely in our court.

As Christians and leaders, we must understand that religious activity and works do not replace intimacy with Christ. He is to be our first work and first love. Out of that love for Him is birthed true works that are anointed.

Christians must beware of replacing a vibrant, energized, intimate relationship with God with going to church, reading so many scriptures per day, getting a certain number of people saved each month, and any other work. These are all important things that we know are *good*, but without our relationship with God, they are simply from the tree of the knowledge of *good* and evil, which results in feeling justified by works instead of by faith in Jesus' finished work of the cross.

With all this said, what are some practical ways to spend time with God? Set apart times of worship. I like to put in an anointed worship CD and raise my hands in worship to Him. During these times, I focus on His goodness and character. I also try to be sensitive to His voice during these times. I also speak praises to Him. Sometimes He leads me to study, read a good book, or listen to a good teaching tape. Other ways to spend time with Him include talking with Him (remember to listen too), writing Him love letters, and reading Him portions of scripture (He loves the psalms). Ask the Holy Spirit to reveal to you ways that you can grow in your relationship with Him.

In today's fast-paced society, we must be especially aware of our walk with God. The cares of this world and busy schedules compete for our time. Wisdom is crying out for us to schedule our time around God not God around our time.

3 SMYRNA

And to the angel of the church of Smyrna write...
(Revelation 2:8)

The city of Smyrna was considered one of the most brilliant cities of ancient Asia Minor even rivaling the great cities of Pergamos and Ephesus. It stood upon a harbor at the head of one of the chief highways to the interior of Asia Minor and was a great trading center and the chief port for export trade until the discovery of America and the resulting discovery of a sea route to India. Smyrna's streets were paved, which was rare in those days, and it was celebrated for its schools of science and medicine.

According to the book of Revelation, the church at Smyrna is considered the persecuted church. It was here that Polycarp, a pupil of John, was martyred in A.D. 155. Scholars believe that his martyrdom was not so much Roman instigated as it was Jewish instigated for Smyrna had a large Jewish population. Smyrna is also considered the city in which emperor worship was developed. Christians throughout the Roman Empire, not just Smyrna, suffered much tribulation for not bowing and calling Caesar "Lord."

The Persecuted Church

In Greek, "Smyrna" comes from a root word that means myrrh.[1] Myrrh is a perfume that exudes spontaneously or by incisions made on a small thorny tree that grows in Arabia and Ethiopia. The myrrh droplets harden into a gum that was used by the ancients in perfumes and incense. Myrrh symbolizes persecution and was one of the gifts laid at Jesus' feet by the wise men, which prophesied of His persecution at the hands of the religious leaders and subsequent crucifixion on the cross (Matt. 2:11).

> And walk in love, as Christ also has loved us and given Himself for us, an offering and a sacrifice to God for a sweet-smelling aroma (Ephesians 5:2).

Jesus gave Himself as an offering to God on our behalf. Just like the incisions made into the thorny tree releases the sweet smell of myrrh, so did Christ's wounds release a sweet aroma to God. Through persecution, the church at Smyrna released the same sweet-smelling aroma. They truly had fellowship with His sufferings and were conformed to His death (Phil. 3:10). I believe this is why the church at Smyrna was one of only two churches that did not receive a rebuke from the resurrected Christ.

> Now thanks be to God who always leads us in triumph in Christ, and through us diffuses the fragrance of His knowledge in every place. For we are to God the fragrance of Christ among those who are being saved and among those who are perishing (2 Cor. 2:14,15).

In the above passage, Paul uses Roman imagery to convey our victory in Christ. A triumph was a Roman victory parade for the conquering army and its leader. As the victorious Roman army proceeded through the streets of Rome, the smell of burning spices filled the air. We are in a war, but unlike the Roman army, we are victorious even if it looks like we've lost on this earth. Our bodies may be torn, beaten, and struck down, but the wounds we sustain in battle (persecution) release a fragrance from us that is left everywhere like the burning spices of the Roman triumph. And at the last day, Christ will raise those of us who have fallen in death and lead us into the final battle to establish His earthly rule.

> So that we ourselves boast of you among the churches of God for your patience and faith in all your **persecutions**

and tribulations that you endure, which is manifest evidence of the righteous judgment of God**, that you may be counted worthy of the kingdom of God,** for which you also suffer (2 Thess. 1:4,5).

For our light affliction, which is but for a moment, is working for us a far more exceeding and eternal weight of glory (2 Cor. 4:18).

For I consider the sufferings of this present time are not worthy to be compared with the glory which shall be revealed in us (Rom. 8:18).

GREETING

These things says the First and the Last, who was dead, and came to life (Revelation 2:8).

The First and the Last, the One who was dead and is now alive. This was a fitting greeting to the persecuted church at Smyrna. Christ quoted from a verse in Isaiah, "Thus says the Lord, the King of Israel, and his Redeemer, the Lord of hosts; 'I am the First and I am the Last; besides Me there is no God'" (Is. 44:6). Christ was declaring to this church that lived in the midst of Caesar worship that He is the only Man who died and came alive again. He is declaring He is the only King and the only God. No Caesar ever died and was resurrected. He is the King of kings, and the Lord of lords. This greeting reinforced and encouraged the church at Smyrna not to bow down to worship Caesar as God nor call Caesar Lord. He also declared Himself as the resurrected Christ giving comfort to those who were alive in Him that the ones who had died and those of them who might die would be raised from the dead.

And do not fear those who kill the body but cannot kill the soul. But rather fear Him who is able to destroy both soul and body in hell (Matt. 10:27).

EXORTATION

I know your works, tribulation, and poverty (but you are rich); and I know the blasphemy of those who say they are Jews and are not, but are a synagogue of Satan (Revelation 2:9).

The word "know" means to understand.[2] As Hebrews 4:15 says, "For we do not have a High Priest who cannot sympathize with our weaknesses, but was in all points tempted as we are, yet without sin." He was letting the persecuted church at Smyrna know that He understood their fears, frustrations, and uncertainty. He bottled their tears and counted every drop as precious when they lost their husbands, children, and friends. He knew how hard it was for them to forgive their persecutors and wept for joy when they did.

"Poverty," which is *ptovhria* in the Greek, comes from a root meaning (*ptokhos*) to crouch, beggar, pauper indicating destitution and indigence.[3] This is in contrast to another Greek word for poverty (*penes*) that means poor but capable of providing for oneself.[4] The idea is that the church at Smyrna was like a poor, destitute beggar in the midst of the beautiful and wealthy city of Smyrna. They were completely helpless to provide for and to deliver themselves from their persecutions. It might also be that they were under financial boycott by their persecutors, yet, Jesus said they are rich for their faith and steadfastness in the midst of persecution (James 2:5).

> And I will say to my soul, "Soul, you have many goods laid up for many years, take your ease; eat, drink, and be merry." But God said to him, "Fool! This night your soul will be required of you; then whose will those things be which you have provided? **So is he who lays up treasure for himself, and is not rich toward God** (Luke 12:19-21).

In reality, the inhabitants of Smyrna, who had great wealth, were the poor ones, the beggars. Their temporal treasures could not pay for entrance into heaven, and at their death, they would stand poor before God. In contrast, the church at Smyrna, who appeared poor to the inhabitants of Smyrna, was rich toward God. They were living the spiritual principle that to lose your life means to gain it, a principle that the apostle Peter had to learn the hard way.

> From that time Jesus began to show to His disciples that He must go to Jerusalem, and suffer many things from the elders and chief priests and scribes, and be killed, and be raised the third day. Then Peter took Him aside and began to rebuke Him, saying, "Far be it from You, Lord; this shall not happen to You!" But He turned and said to Peter, "Get behind Me, Satan! You are an offense to Me, **for you are not mindful of the things of God, but the things of men**" (Matt. 16:21-23).

Peter had his mind on the things of men. He still did not understand the purpose behind Christ's suffering and death and how important it was. For the Christ, the Son of God to suffer and die on a cross was unthinkable!

> Then Jesus said to His disciples, "If anyone desires to come after Me, let him deny himself, and take up his cross, and follow Me. For whoever desires to save his life will lose it, but whoever loses his life for My sake will find it. For what **profit** is it to a man if **he gains the whole world, and loses his soul?** Or what will a man give in exchange for his soul? For the Son of Man will come in the glory of His Father with His angels, and then He will reward each according to his works (Matt. 17:24-27).

Christ, the God of the universe with immeasurable riches, became poor for us (Phil. 2:5-8). Remember, our God knows what wealth is; everything is His, and He understands profit and loss. He was saying that it is a severe loss for a man to gain the whole world and lose his soul. Can that man give Christ, who owns everything, all his wealth in exchange for his soul at Christ's appearing? No!

Peter later lived this principle. Tradition states that he was killed in Rome by crucifixion. He asked that he be crucified upside down because he was not worthy to die the same way his Lord died. Some even say that when he saw the place of his death, he said, "Oh, beloved cross, how I have longed for thee."

Synagogue of Satan

Jesus also stated that He knew "the blasphemy of those who say they are Jews and are not." This was an intense rebuke toward the Jewish population. At that time, they still met in synagogues as they had done for hundreds of years. They did not believe that Jesus was the long-awaited Messiah, and for this reason, they persecuted the Christians. As a matter of fact, scholars believe that in Smyrna the Jews were more antagonistic than even the Romans!

The Jews were nationalistic and proud of their race with its rich history and separatism. However, Jesus declares that they are not Jews. What a rebuke! Jesus, while on this earth, told the Jewish leaders that they did the deeds of their father. They boldly declared that they had one Father—God. But Jesus declared that their father was the devil because of the murder and deceit in their hearts. He is continuing this theme in speaking to the church at Smyrna. Paul explains, "For he is not a Jew who is one outwardly, nor is circumcision that which is outward in the flesh; but he is a Jew who is one inwardly; and circumcision is that of the heart, in the Spirit, not in the letter; whose praise is not from men but from God" (Rom. 2:28, 29). Everyone who is born again is a Jew even though Gentile by blood. The Jewish population at Smyrna was persecuting the true Jews.

Jesus then called them "a synagogue of Satan," which is a play on words from Numbers 16:3 where Korah called the Israelites in the wilderness "the assembly of the Lord." Synagogue and assembly both mean congregation. Korah led a rebellion against Moses, who was a type of Christ. He felt that Moses exalted himself by taking too much responsibility of leading the people. He declared that all the congregation was holy not just Moses. Even though Korah spoke on behalf of the congregation of the Israelites, he coveted Moses' position just like Satan coveted God's position. Korah's rebellion resulted in judgment upon himself and those who followed him (Nu. 16:1-33).

This same spirit of rebellion operated in the Jews of Jesus' and the early church's time. When Christ came, a tremendous shift occurred in which the presence of God ceased dwelling among the nation of Israel and began to dwell in individuals. Israel did not understand that they foreshadowed a future spiritual nation made up of many different people groups joined together by one bloodline—Christ's. This is why the Bible says that when we get saved, we are a new creation or race. They were invited to become a part of this new race, but their lack of understanding blinded them to this truth. Therefore, they persecuted the Lord and His followers. But the Jews are not without hope. The Bible explains that they were blinded for our (Gentiles) sake, and one day "all Israel will be saved" (Rom. 11:26). *All* does not mean every single Jew but the majority. I believe that a massive revival of the Jewish people will occur before Christ's second return and that this will be a sign of His soon return.

There is a false doctrine that says Jews are not required to be "born again" or "saved" as non-Jews are, but Christ was clear. He stated to Nicodemus, a pious Jew, that you must be born again of the Spirit in order to enter the kingdom of God (Jn. 3:1-5). Jesus also taught His Jewish followers that anyone who wanted to be saved must enter through Him because He is the door (Jn. 10:7, 9). In another place, He said that no one comes to the Father except through Him (Jn. 14:6). At the end, Christ will unite the two—the saved physical Jews to the saved spiritual Jews.

> And other sheep I have which are not of this fold; them also I must bring, and they will hear My voice; and there will be **one flock and one shepherd** (Jn. 10:16).

Older Brother Versus the Younger Brother

As this age comes to a close, we will see more betrayals between fellow Christians, and I believe these betrayals will be motivated by the same religious spirit that motivated the Jews of Jesus' time to persecute Him and His followers. When Jesus' disciples asked Him what was the sign of His coming, He said that one sign was offense, betrayal, and hatred of one another (Mt. 24:10). You see, the enemy knows that a kingdom, house, or city divided against itself cannot stand (Mt. 12:25). For this reason, his goal is to cause Christians to be offended with each other. We can already see this happening in our time. I would venture to say that the majority of Christians who attend church regularly are offended with more than one person in their church, and, sadly, it is often their pastor or others in leadership. If this offense isn't dealt with, it will lead to hatred, which John said is murder (1 Jn. 3:15). We must not be ignorant of the enemy's schemes for he has been dividing brothers since the beginning.

> Now Adam knew Eve his wife, and she conceived and bore Cain, and said, "I have acquired a man from the Lord." Then she bore again, this time his brother Abel. Now Abel was a keeper of sheep, but Cain was a tiller of the ground (Gen. 4:1, 2).

Cain and Abel were the first children born to Adam and Eve after the fall, which means they were born with a sinful nature in the image of Adam (Gen. 5:3). Eve named her firstborn Cain because she had acquired a man from the Lord. "Man" is an interesting Hebrew word *ish*. *Ish* is a man, husband, male, an individual person.[5] It is one of four Hebrew words used for man. *Adam* is the generic term for human or mankind, which can include both male and female.[6] *Ish* conveys a sense of nobility, strength, and social standing much like the word gentleman conveys in English societies. *Ish* is often paired with *ishah*, the name for wife. God expresses His desire to be a husband to His people when He said in Hosea 2:16 that His people would one day no longer call Him, "My Master," but would instead call Him, "My Husband (*ish*)."

"Acquired" is another interesting word, which is akin to the name of Cain. "Acquired" means to erect, that is, create; by extension to procure. It also means purchase, recover, and redeem.[7] Cain means "*fixity*; a *lance* (as *striking fast*):-spear," but it also has an affinity to "acquired."[8] As I studied the meaning of these words, I began to perceive that Eve put a lot of hope in Cain.

After the fall, God told the serpent that enmity would exist between him and the woman and her Seed and his seed. He prophesied that the Seed would bruise his head, and Satan would bruise the Seed's heal. "Bruise" means to crush,[9] and "head" means chief, leader, or headship.[10] When Adam and Eve submitted to Satan and disobeyed God, they handed over their headship to him. God said that the Seed would crush his headship or rule on this earth. Jesus was obviously the Seed. However, neither Eve nor Satan knew who the Seed was. I believe that

Eve hoped Cain was the seed that God had talked about. Another interesting tidbit that supports this is the name Abel. *Abel* literally means breath or nothing. How would you like to be named Nothing? I believe that Eve thought Abel was unnecessary since she had Cain, the firstborn and, hopefully, the Seed. All her hopes and dreams for redemption were upon Cain. However, the Bible tells us that after Cain killed Abel, she realized that Abel had been of the true Seed even though he wasn't the Seed Himself.

> And Adam knew his wife again, and she bore a son and named him Seth, "For God has appointed another seed for me instead of Abel, whom Cain killed" (Gen. 4:25).

Even though Seth was not the Seed, he was the seed that carried the Seed. In other words, through his bloodline, Jesus the Messiah came (Lk. 3:38). It is from Seth's line that man began to call on the name of the Lord (Gen. 4:26).

There was another person who believed that Cain might be the Seed—Satan. He sought to destroy Cain and Abel from the beginning. I believe that Cain opened the door to Satan through pride that had sprouted and grown to maturity. Imagine as a child your parents telling you of their mistake, but that God promised a Seed, which could be you! And you're a good boy. You're the older brother and more responsible. You are a hard worker, a tiller of the ground, unlike your kid brother who watches after sheep. He even gets to nap in the heat of the day. Not you. You are too busy farming in the heat of the day to slow down. Yep, you are the apple of your mother's eye. And, as the older brother, you are used to getting your own way. You have more privileges. You are a leader. You initiated the offering to the Lord. But then something happens that shatters your self-image. All of a sudden you are rejected.

> And in the process of time it came to pass that Cain brought an offering of the fruit of the ground to the Lord. Abel also brought of the firstborn of his flock and of their fat. And the Lord respected Abel and his offering, but He did not respect Cain and his offering. And Cain was very angry, and his countenance fell (Gen. 4:3-5).

To understand what happened, we need to look at a few things in this passage. First, Cain brought the fruit of the ground, and Abel brought the firstborn of his flock and their fat, which means that he offered more than one sheep. How did Abel know to bring the firstborn and how did he know to offer their fat? Long after Cain and Abel, Moses wrote in Leviticus 3:16 that the fat was the Lord's. Abel might have learned that a blood sacrifice is pleasing to God from the fact that God killed an animal and clothed his parents in its skins (Gen. 3:21), but that still doesn't explain the fat offering. Unless God had told his parents this, Abel must have learned this by divine inspiration, which implies that he was a praying man.

Second, Cain's offering was from his labor, but Abel's was from his faith. Cain's offering represented religious works. Religion says you must keep all the rules (praying a certain way or length, reading your Bible each day, going to church each service, feeding the poor, etc.) in order to be justified by God. Religion tries to gain God's favor on its own terms instead of God's terms, which is exalting the religious person's will over God's will. Satan tried this and was kicked out of heaven (Isaiah 14:13-14). Religion is trusting in the flesh instead of in God. On the other hand, Abel's offering was by faith. He didn't labor as much as his brother, but he was obedient in continuing the precedent God began by sacrificing the animal to clothe his parents (Gen. 3:21).

Third, God's reaction wasn't what Cain expected. "Respected" means to inspect, consider, or gaze at, but it has a far more revealing meaning. It also means to look around in amazement.[11] Try to picture what occurred when Abel offered his sheep. God sees this awesome act of faith, the first since the fall, and looks around at all those gathered in His throne room in amazement. It is the "drop-jaw syndrome." When something unbelievable happens to you, your mouth drops open in amazement, and you are looking at everyone to see if they saw what you just saw. This is what God did. He was absolutely amazed to see faith in fallen man.

Cain was also amazed but not at Abel's faith. He was amazed that God would accept his baby brother's offering over his own! How could this be? Cain had worked harder. Had God overlooked the fact that he might be the Seed? God's rejection of him and his offering brought to the surface Cain's pride and arrogance. It also revealed that faith not religion pleases God. Cain had put too much confidence in his abilities and position in the family. For this reason, he couldn't handle God's rejection, and he was very angry. This wasn't a typical anger. I believe this anger was the same as what the older brother of the prodigal experienced when his father accepted his wayward son back into the family after years of riotous living (Lk 15:11-32). This anger is a furious passion and a raging desire for revenge. It is so intense that it can only be terminated with killing the object of its wrath. And, as we all know, Cain did exactly that (Gen. 4:8).

Finally, the story of Cain and Abel is prophetic of the last days. The phrase in Genesis 4:3, "in the process of time" literally means "at the end of days." We know that Cain and Abel didn't live at the end of days but at the beginning. However, I believe God used this phrase to warn us to guard our hearts against a stronghold of religion that smothers faith. In Luke 18:8, Jesus asked, "Nevertheless, when the Son of Man comes, will He really find faith on the earth?" The story of Cain and Abel reveals that religion and faith are hostile to each other. The enmity that God said would be between Satan's seed and His Seed continues today. We are of the Seed, and the religious are of the enemy's. Both have been maturing and will have a final confrontation before Christ's return.

> For I have bent Judah, My bow, fitted the bow with Ephraim, and raised up your sons, O Zion, against your sons, O Greece, and made you like the sword of a mighty man (Zechariah 9:13).

This scripture is speaking of a battle between the sons of Zion and the sons of Greece. The sons of Zion are the true sons and daughters of God. Zion means permanent capital and is a mountain in Jerusalem. It is at Zion that David brought the ark of God, and it became a central place of worship until the first temple was built. However, Zion is still God's permanent capital or dwelling place except today it is a spiritual place instead of physical (Heb. 12:22). True worshipers worship God in Spirit and in truth on His holy mount called Zion (Jn. 4:23).

"Greece" is *yavan* in Hebrew and means effervescing (that is, hot and active).[12] Scholars believe it is probably the same as another Hebrew word, *yayin*, that means "to *effervesce*; *wine* (as fermented); by implication *intoxication*."[13] According to the dictionary, ferment is a substance such as yeast or bacteria that causes fermentation. Synonyms of fermentation include effervescence, excitement, agitation, turbulence, frothing, and seething.[14]

> Then Jesus said to them, "Take heed, and beware of the leaven of the Pharisees and the Sadducees...Then they (disciples) understood that He did not tell them to beware of the leaven of bread, but of the doctrine of the Pharisees and Sadducees (Matthew 16:6, 12).

Another word for leaven is yeast, and it means *ferment* in the Greek.[15] Keeping in mind that sons of Greece can be understood as "sons of ferment," and that Jesus said to beware of the leaven or ferment of the Pharisees (religious) and Herod (political), we can safely say that the sons of Greece are religious and political leaders that resist the leaven of the kingdom and Jesus Christ. You see, the religious may despise the world leaders, but they will use them for their own means just as the Pharisees used the Roman leaders to crucify Christ. They are always in a state of agitation, excitement, and turbulence. They have no peace. And I believe that these sons of Greece are in Christian circles today and attend the same churches the sons of Zion attend. These are the religious who live under the Law of works and despise the true sons of Zion who live by faith. These have a heart of Cain and an appearance of godliness, but they are actually white washed sepulchers full of deadmen's bones (unclean). They despise the true because the true live the life they are trying so hard to work for, and the true threaten their very existence. They think they are right and no amount of persuasion will change their minds. Like the Jews of old who persecuted the true Son of Zion, **the sons of Greece at the end of days will betray and persecute the true sons of Zion**.

> And then many will be offended, will **betray** one another, and will hate one another (Matt. 24:10).

Here is one more tidbit from the story of Cain and Abel. Remember that one meaning of Cain is spear. What pierced Christ's side?

> Therefore, because it was the Preparation Day, that the bodies should not remain on the cross on the Sabbath (for that Sabbath was a high day), the Jews asked Pilate that their legs might be broken, and that they might be taken away. Then the soldiers came and broke the legs of the first and of the other who was crucified with Him. But when they came to Jesus and saw that the He was already dead, they did not break His legs. But one of the soldiers pierced His side with a **spear**, and immediately blood and water came out (John 19:31-34).

Even though it was a Roman who pierced His side with a spear, according to Zechariah 12:10, it was the Israelites who actually pierced Him.

> And I will pour on **the house of David and on the inhabitants of Jerusalem** the Spirit of grace and supplication; then they will look on Me whom they pierced. Yes, they will mourn for Him as one mourns for his only son and grieve for Him as one grieves for a firstborn.

The religious of Jesus' time (at the beginning of the end of days) used a Roman spear and struck the True so that they could keep their feasts and Sabbath according to the Law. It is the story of Cain and Abel all over again. However, Zechariah 12:10 gives us hope and prophesies of the future salvation of Israel when grace and supplication will be poured out upon them so that they will mourn the One they had rejected.

THE PROMISE

> Do not fear any of those things which you are about to suffer. Indeed, the devil is about to throw some of you into prison, that you may be tested, and you will have tribulation ten days. Be faithful until death, and I will give you the crown of life (Revelation 2:10).

What a prophetic word! Can you imagine going to a church service desiring to hear a prophetic word from God and receiving one like this! I think that would convince some to never want another prophetic word again. Or some would think it was a curse from the enemy and rebuke it or ignore it. Even so, Jesus strengthened their resolve by telling them exactly what was going to happen **and** by telling them their reward.

Notice that Jesus said the **devil** was going to persecute them. The reason Jesus could easily forgive His persecutors is because He knew that it was the Evil One manipulating them (Jn. 13:27). He also saw beyond the persecution to the divine destiny He was fulfilling. Jesus commands us not to fear the things that we suffer for His sake. The word "fear" is *phobeo* in the Greek, and it means to be frightened of, to be exceedingly afraid, to be alarmed, or to be in awe of. [16] In this context, we can understand that Jesus was telling them not to be alarmed or frightened. But I also think it is interesting that the word fear also means to be in awe of. The enemy tries to get us in awe of him by the things he does to us. Awe can also mean terror or dread. The enemy purposely tries to make us dread each day and weigh us down with worries or anxieties by manipulating circumstances and people to accomplish his plans of death and destruction.

> For consider Him who endured such hostility from sinners against Himself, lest you become weary and discouraged in your souls. You have not yet resisted to bloodshed, striving against sin. And you have forgotten the exhortation which speaks to you as to sons: "My son, do not despise the chastening [discipline] of the Lord, nor be discouraged when you are rebuked by Him; for whom the Lord loves He chastens, and scourges [to flog, whip] every son whom He receives." If you endure chastening, God deals with you as sons; for what son is there whom a father does not chasten? But if you are without chastening, of which we all have become partakers, then you are illegitimate [bastards] and not sons (Heb. 12:3-8).

You must settle this in your heart—God disciplines, chastens, and scourges His children. Often His rod of correction is the enemy working through people. We can liken it to using a paddle to spank a child. The paddle is the tool used to discipline the child. The child despises the paddle because he knows it inflicts pain. The parent doesn't like the paddle either, but the parent understands its use as a tool. The same is true of the relationship between God and the devil. If God doesn't discipline us through unfair treatment, persecution, and trials, we would be spoiled, prideful, stiff-necked, rebellious children. As a matter of fact, I am concerned for any Christian that God is not disciplining especially if they are backslidden or sinning.

> For they (earthly fathers) indeed for a few days chastened us as seemed best to them, but He for our profit, that we may be partakers of His holiness. Now no chastening seems to be joyful for the present, but painful; nevertheless, afterward it yields the peaceable fruit of righteousness to those who have been trained by it (Heb. 12:10,11).

God's correction is a good thing and much needed for our transformation process. God chastens us so that we might be sharers and companions of His holiness, without which no one will see the Lord (Heb. 12:14). He knows better than we do that His chastening produces in us the fruit of righteousness. There is a wrong mindset in the church today that we can live however we want and still dwell with God in heaven when we die. The Bible is clear—you must be holy as He is holy (1 Pet. 1:15,16). This doesn't mean that we will not still have areas in our life that need changing when we die, but it does mean that we should be aggressively working with the Holy Spirit to be changed into the image of Christ (Rom. 8:29).

Jesus stated that the troubles that were going to come upon the church in Smyrna would last for ten days. Why? The number ten often represents testimony in the Bible. The church at Smyrna was going to be a testimony of the faithfulness of Christ to their accusers and persecutors. But how can we be a testimony if we're beaten, scourged, thrown into prison, and even killed? First, we must look at the whole of the Bible. Wasn't Joseph a testimony everywhere he went whether as a slave or in prison? Wasn't David a testimony when Saul was persecuting him? Wasn't Elijah a testimony? Wasn't John the Baptist? Wasn't Jesus of

Nazareth? You see, all of these were persecuted and lived under much hardship; yet, they spoke of God's faithfulness and kindness. Can you imagine how Joseph felt when he interpreted the baker's and the cupbearer's dreams, and his dreams seemed like a cruel joke? Remember, the thorny bush must be marred and cut before it exudes the fragrance of myrrh.

> And walk in love, as Christ also has loved us and given Himself for us, an offering and a sacrifice to God **for a sweet smelling aroma** (Eph. 5:2).

The Crown of Life

> Be faithful until death, and I will give you the crown of life. He who has an ear, let him hear what the Spirit says to the churches. He who overcomes shall not be hurt by the second death (Rev. 2:10b,11).

The word "crown" is *stephanos*, which is also the Greek word for Stephen, the first Christian martyr (Acts 8:54-60).[17]

> Do you not know that those who run in a race all run, but one receives the prize? Run in such a way that you may obtain it. And everyone who competes for the prize is temperate in all things. Now they do it to obtain a perishable crown, but we for an imperishable crown (1 Cor. 9:24,25).

> Blessed is the man who endures temptation; for when he has been approved, he will receive the crown of life which the Lord has promised to those who love Him (James 1:12).

How do we overcome? By falling in love with Him because only then will we be willing to die for Him. By love, I am not talking of a *phileo* love in which we have affection for Him. Many in today's churches believe that is love for Him. I am talking about a love that is born only through intimacy with Him, an *agape* love.

The next part of the promise is that those who overcome shall not be hurt by the second death. Those who are part of the catching away at His second return are part of the first resurrection in which those who are dead in Christ are resurrected, and those who are alive and remain are changed into incorruptible (1 Thess. 4:13-17). These will live and rule with Christ for 1,000 years after His return. After the thousand years, Satan will be loosed from his prison to deceive the nations one last time, and then he is thrown into the lake of fire and brimstone to be tormented day and night forever (Rev. 20:7-10). After this, the great white throne judgment occurs in which the dead that were not part of the first resurrection stand before God. Anyone not found written in the Lamb's Book of Life is thrown into the lake of fire, and, finally, death and Hades are thrown in also (Rev. 20:11-15). According to Christ, those who are faithful and overcome shall not be hurt by this second death, but instead will be part of the first resurrection. You see, there are two resurrections: the catching away and the second death. Which one do you wish to be a part of?

> But the rest of the dead did not live again until the thousand years were finished. This is the first resurrection. Blessed and holy is he who has part in the first resurrection. Over such the second death has no power, but they shall be priests of God and of Christ, and shall reign with Him a thousand years (Rev. 20:5,6).

We have a choice to make—do we want to suffer here temporarily or later permanently? This choice is hard to make in the Western society we live in, especially with the freedoms we enjoy. Death, suffering, persecution, and testing are not popular subjects in the Western church. There are some who teach that God doesn't want us to go through these things, but that is completely against God's word. My pastor once said that any true doctrine can be taught anywhere in the world. Can the doctrine that we are not supposed to suffer be preached to those Christians in Muslim countries that are dying for their faith everyday? Can the doctrine that every Christian is supposed to be rich be taught to believers in India? Examine any teaching in light of the Word and if it can be preached to anyone in the world.

APPLICATION

The message delivered to the church at Smyrna almost 2,000 years ago is relevant to the church today, especially in countries that persecute Christians. Even though Christians are not as persecuted for their faith in America and much of the Western church to the extent of other nations, we can still use every trial and hardship for training. For example, when we are treated unfairly, use it as an opportunity for cleansing your heart and loving the one who hurt you. When you are stuck in a traffic jam or long line at the store, use that as an opportunity to exercise your fruit of patience (patience is ONLY developed during trials). When you are misunderstood, shunned, ignored, talked about, and rejected, use those times for pressing into more of God and His presence. And rejoice because you are in good company. Not only did all the greats in the Bible experience these same things but the High Priest, Jesus Christ, did too (Heb. 2:18). Make up your mind today to embrace God's chastening in whatever form and to excel in whatever testing or persecution you experience.

And, finally, grow in *agape* love. The first commandment is to love God with our entire being, and out of that relationship we will love our neighbor (Mt. 22:37-40). We will also gain eternal vision. By this I mean that Christ will become the center of our vision or focus. The thought of sharing in His suffering becomes an honor (Phil. 3:10, 11), and in the face of death, we will feel anticipation in being in our Savior's arms shortly. Remember, there can't be a resurrection unless there is a death.

> For I consider the sufferings of this present time are not worthy to be compared with the glory which shall be revealed in us (Rom. 8:18).

> That I may know Him and the power of His resurrection, and the fellowship of His sufferings, being conformed to His death, if, by any means, I may attain to the resurrection from the dead (Phil. 3:10, 11).

4 PERGAMOS

And to the angel of the church in Pergamos write... (Revelation 2:12).

Pergamos was a city in the province Mysia located in northwest Asia Minor. Pergamos was famous for two things: its massive library containing 200,000 volumes (rolls) and its idolatry. In Pergamos alone, there were temples for the four "great" gods of Zeus (god of sky or weather), Dionysus (god of ecstasy or wine), Athena (god of protection of cities), and Asklepios (god of medicine) and three temples dedicated to Roman emperors. Pergamos was considered a religious center in the Roman Empire, and the center of emperor worship. It is here that the famed altar of Zeus was located and was considered one of the wonders of the ancient world.

"Pergamos" means citadel in the Greek.[1] According to *Webster's New World Dictionary and Thesaurus,* a citadel is a "fortress on a commanding height for defense of a city, a fortified place; stronghold." A synonym for citadel is castle. Rulers live in castles and sit on thrones.

I know your works, and where you dwell, where Satan's **throne** is... (Rev. 2:13).

The word throne denotes authority. It is obvious from Pergamos' history, that it was a stronghold or citadel of idol worship and Satan had great authority here. What is also interesting is that the altar of Zeus overlooked Pergamos. Remember that citadel also means a "fortress on a commanding **height** for defense of a city." For those who are unfamiliar with the demonic realm, the enemy places rulers, principalities, and powers over cities, towns, and countries to propagate his purposes and to defend his territory (Dan. 10:10-20; Eph. 6:12). The altar of Zeus overlooking this city is a physical manifestation of the spiritual ruler of the city. Human sacrifices were conducted on this throne.

In 1923, the Germans excavated the Biblical city of Pergamos and placed their finds in the Pergamos Museum located in Berlin. One find that was put on display there is "Satan's throne," the very throne of Zeus that oversaw the city of Pergamos. Hitler later had a replica of "Satan's throne" built at his "spiritual capital" of Nuremberg. This throne oversaw the large parade ground where he held some of his rallies. The Pergamos Museum in Berlin survived the war and "Satan's throne" is there to this day.[2]

EXORTATION

> These things says He who has the sharp two-edged sword. I know your works, and where you dwell, where Satan's throne is. And you hold fast to My name, and did not deny My faith even in the days in which Antipas was My faithful martyr, who was killed among you, where Satan dwells. (Revelation 2:12b, 13).

Pergamos was extremely hostile territory for Christians to live in; yet, they held fast to Christ's name and did not deny the faith even though it meant sure death. In fact, each year there was a "festival" to honor and worship Caesar as God. The whole city would march to the temple and were forced to declare Caesar as Lord and God. According to scholars, any who refused were killed at the altar. One example is Antipas who according to tradition was thrown into the altar and roasted when he refused to worship Caesar. When Jesus said that they had held fast to His name, He wasn't talking about just His name but also His authority. In the ancient Greek, *name* also means authority, which sheds new light on the scripture in Philippians 2:10

> "Therefore God also has highly exalted Him and given Him the name which is above every name, that at the name of Jesus every knee should bow, of those in heaven and of those on earth, and of those under the earth."

This verse could say, God has "given Him the **authority** which is above every **authority**...that at the **authority** of Jesus every knee should bow." In a place where Satan reigned through his various "gods," these Christians held fast to the one true Authority. They knew Caesar was only a man and that his and Satan's authority in Pergamos and the world was temporary. They refused to bow the knee to anyone but the Lord. We need to understand this also especially as the world grows darker. Jesus acknowledged Satan's authority on this earth (Jn. 14:30), but He also came to destroy his works (1 Jn. 3:8b). This destruction of Satan's rule over the earth is continuing and will continue through the works of the Christians. You could say that Jesus "got the ball rolling," but we are the ones that are to enforce the work He accomplished and gradually consume all other kingdoms (Dan. 2:44). In the meantime, Christ will continue to sit upon His throne ruling His kingdom through the hearts of His people until all His enemies are His footstool (1 Cor. 15:25).

False Teachers and Doctrines

> But I have a few things against you, because you have there those who hold the doctrine of Balaam, who taught Balak to put a stumbling block before the children of Israel, to eat things sacrificed to idols, and to commit sexual immorality. Thus you also have those who hold the doctrine of the Nicolaitans, which thing I hate (Rev. 2:14,15).

In the church at Pergamos, there were two false doctrines at work: the doctrine of Balaam and the doctrine of the Nicolaitans. Scholars are not sure what these doctrines consisted of, but we do know that whatever was taught, the Lord hated it. Some suggest the doctrine of the Balaam might have been tied in with the worship of the Dionysus, the goddess of wine and ecstasy. The worship of this goddess was so vulgar and immoral and full of drunken sexual deviance that even Rome outlawed it. At one part in the festivities, the worshipers gorged themselves on raw meat dedicated to Dionysus. Notice that the doctrine of the Balaam involved sacrificing to idols and sexual immorality. His rebuke was that the church was allowing those who held and taught these doctrines to remain as part of the congregation. Could it be some were combining aspects of this idol worship with Christianity? Or were they proclaiming to be Christians but also taking part of the festivities? We don't know, but the correlation is intriguing.

Any doctrine or teaching that is contrary to the gospel and the written Word is to be dismissed. Paul instructed believers to shun profane and idle babblings because they lead to more ungodliness, and they spread quickly (1 Tim. 6:20). He even named two men who were spreading false doctrine at that time so that they would not deceive others (2 Tim. 2:16-18). In Galatians 2:11-14, which mostly deals with false doctrine, Paul described publicly rebuking the Apostle Peter for straying from the truth! He also rebuked the Galatians for believing a false gospel over the truth.

> I marvel that you are turning away so soon from Him who called you in the grace of Christ, **to a different gospel, which is not another,** but there are some who trouble you and want to pervert the gospel of Christ. But even if we or an angel from heaven, preach any other gospel to you than what we have preached to you, let him be accursed (Gal. 1:6-8).

There are absolutes in the Bible such as the deity of Christ, His virgin birth, His death, burial and resurrection, the trinity, the atonement of the blood, etc. But there are some things that are not absolutes such as should Christians vote, where to live, what church to go to, celebrating Christmas, etc. Any doctrine that is against the absolutes of the Bible is false. In the above scriptures, Paul spoke of the Christians turning from Christ "to a different gospel, which is not another." Initially, I didn't understand this until I looked up the Greek words. "Different" means another of a different kind.[3] "Another" means another of the same kind.[4]

Jesus used "another" when He said that He would pray to the Father to give us "another Helper" (Jn. 14:16). He was saying that He would ask the Father to send another of the same kind or like Him to help us during His absence. "Gospel" simply means a good message,[5] and all true Christian messages will be of the same kind as the Word. Anything that goes against the Word is a gospel of a different kind and should be rejected. A good indicator of a different gospel is if it promotes sin and fleshly living. These messages often tickle the flesh instead of challenging the individual to come up higher spiritually, or they assuage the guilt of the flesh for not living right by following laws.

In light of this false doctrine in the Pergamos church, it is not a coincidence that one of the first things Jesus says to Christians there was, "...these things says He who has the sharp two-edged sword" (Rev. 2:12b).

> And take the helmet of salvation, and **the sword of the Spirit, which is the word of God** (Eph. 6:17).

> **For the word of God is living and powerful, and sharper than any two-edged sword**, piercing even to the division of soul and spirit, and of joints and marrow, and is a discerner of the thoughts and intents of the heart (Heb. 4:12).

The Word is the only effective weapon against false doctrines. As Christians, we must become rooted in the Word so that we can recognize any false doctrines taught today. Many of those who teach false doctrines either do so unknowingly because they are teaching messages they have heard but haven't studied themselves, or they teach false messages knowingly for control and material gain. In both cases, the teacher of false doctrine is often a Christian, someone who acts like a Christian, or someone who was once a Christian. These individuals know the language and lifestyle of Christians and act accordingly in Christian circles, which is why true discernment is imperative in these last days.

A side note on the "sharp two-edged sword" is fascinating. In Pergamos, the governor was granted unusual authority in which he could order the death penalty using a two-edged sword. Like any Jewish Rabbi, the Lord used everyday customs, objects, and examples the people could relate to. He was reminding His people that He is the true King with all authority who carries the true two-edged sword.

The Doctrine of Balaam

As stated above, the doctrine of Balaam could have been tied in with the worship of Dionysus, but I feel it's important to look into the Biblical story of Balaam and glean any lessons we can from his story. During the Israelites journey in the wilderness, they came to rest in the plains of Moab. Balak, the king of the Moabites, "saw all that Israel had done to the Amorites. And Moab was exceedingly afraid of the people because they were many, and Moab was sick with dread because of the children of Israel" (Nu. 22:2,3). The Israelites did not come into the plains of Moab to engage in battle. They were simply camped there. The king of Balak sent messengers to a prophet named Balaam that resided at Pethor explaining the situation and asking him to come curse the Israelites.

> Then he sent messengers to Balaam..."Look, a people has come from Egypt. See, they cover the face of the earth, and are settling next to me! Therefore please come at once, curse this people for me. Perhaps I shall be able to defeat them and drive them out of the land, for I know that he whom you bless is blessed, and he whom you curse is cursed" (Nu. 22:5,6).

Balak understood a principle that today's Christians have lost: there is power in the tongue. He knew that if the Israelites were cursed, he could defeat them. Balak promised Balaam a diviner's fee if he would come curse the Israelites. Balaam instructed them to stay the night while he sought the Lord's will on the matter. Sought the Lord's will? What was there to seek?

> Then God came to Balaam and said, "Why are these men with you" (Nu. 22:9)?

When God asks a question, He is not looking for answers. Instead, it is a tool meant to cause us to examine ourselves.

> So Balaam said to God, "Balak the son of Zippor, king of Moab, has sent to me, saying, 'Look, a people has come out of Egypt, and they cover the face of the earth. Come now, curse them for me; perhaps I shall be able to overpower them and drive them out.'" And God said to Balaam, "You shall not go with them; you shall not curse the people, for they are blessed" (Nu. 22:10-12).

Balaam had his answer, but notice how he phrased his answer to the messengers, "Go back to your land, for **the Lord has refused to give me permission to go with you**" (Nu. 22:13). His response brings to my mind of when I was a child and wanted to do something, but my parents wouldn't let me. I would tell my friends that my parents said no while letting them know by my tone and the way I framed my answer that I didn't agree and regretted that I couldn't do what I wanted. This is a subtle form of rebellion. I had an outward appearance of obedience; yet, my heart was far from submitting to the wisdom and knowledge of my parents. This rebellion was in Balaam's heart, and I believe he coveted the diviner's fee. Why else would he even consider Balak's request?

The messengers returned to Moab with Balaam's answer. Balak decided to send princes more numerous and honorable than the first with more promises of a greater reward.

> And they came to Balaam and said to him, "Thus says Balak the son of Zippor: 'Please let nothing hinder you from coming to me; for I will certainly honor you greatly, and I will do whatever you say to me. Therefore please come, curse this people for me'" (Nu. 22:16,17).

Talk about dangling a carrot in front of a rabbit's nose! This carrot was a carrot of wealth, authority, and position.

> "Then Balaam answered and said to the servants of Balak, "Though Balak were to give me his house full of silver and gold, I could not go beyond the word of the Lord my God, to do less or more. Now therefore, please, you also stay here tonight, that I may know what more the Lord will say to me." And God came to Balaam at

night and said to him, "If the men come to call you, rise and go with them; but only the word which I speak to you--that you shall do." So Balaam rose in the morning, saddled his donkey, and went with the princes of Moab (Nu. 22:18-21).

Wait a minute! Didn't God tell Balaam he couldn't go? Why is he telling him that he can go now? First, we need to understand Balaam's desire to go to Balak was tremendous. Notice that Balaam tells the princes that he can't go beyond God's word, but then he tells them to stay the night while he seeks the Lord more on this matter. God already told him that he couldn't go. At this point, the desire for the reward became an idol. Read the following astonishing verses:

> Son of man, these men have set up their idols in their hearts, and put before them that which causes them to stumble into iniquity. **Should I let Myself be inquired of at all by them?** Therefore speak to them, and say to them, "Thus says the Lord God: 'Everyone of the house of Israel who sets up his idols in his heart, and puts before him what causes him to stumble into iniquity, and then comes to the prophet, **I the Lord will answer him who comes according to the multitude of his idols...**And if the prophet is induced to speak anything, I the Lord have induced that prophet, and I will stretch out My hand against him and destroy him from My people Israel'" (Eze. 14:3,4,9).

Read the King James and the Amplified Bible versions of Eze. 14:9:

> And if the prophet be deceived when he hath spoken a thing, **I the LORD have deceived that prophet,** and I will stretch out my hand upon him, and will destroy him from the midst of my people Israel.

> But if the prophet does give the man the answer he desires [thus allowing himself to be a party to the

inquirer's sin of **idolatry**], **I the Lord will see to it that the prophet is deceived in his answer.**

Wow! Do you understand what this means? Our hearts will answer us according to the idols set up there. This explains why some Christians swear God told them to leave their spouses for their adulterous partners. God would never tell anyone to divorce their spouse for their adulterous partner. However, I believe that the deception is serious enough for them to believe that He would tell them something that is contrary to His nature.

Second Chronicles 18 is an example of idols answering an inquiry of God. Ahab asked Jehoshaphat to go to battle with him against Ramoth Gilead. Jehoshaphat wanted to inquire of the Lord before he made his final decision. Ahab gathered all the prophets together to "prophesy" the Lord's will. They all prophesied peace and victory for Jehoshaphat and Ahab if they went into battle, but Jehoshaphat recognized the need for a real prophet.

> But Jehoshaphat said, "Is there not still a prophet of the Lord here, that we may inquire of Him?" So the king of Israel said to Jehoshaphat, "There is still one man by whom we may inquire of the Lord; **but I hate him, because he never prophesies good concerning me, but always evil.** He is Micaiah the son of Imla." And Jehoshaphat said, "Let not the king say such things" (2 Chro. 18:6,7).

King Ahab would rather listen to false prophets and be deceived than heed the voice of a true prophet. It doesn't make sense. Why would someone want to knowingly be lied to? King Ahab was an idolatrous king determined to fulfill his own desires. When we have idols, we don't want to hear the truth because it exposes our motives and requires us to choose life or death (Heb. 4:12). It's the "head in the sand" syndrome. As long as we don't know the truth, we can continue in our deception without harm, but this in itself is deception.

Reluctantly, the king sent for Micaiah, and at first, Micaiah prophesied just like the other prophets. However, Ahab knew this wasn't the truth, and demanded that Micaiah speak the truth (2 Chr. 18:12-15). Read what Micaiah said to the two kings:

> Then Micaiah said, "Therefore hear the word of the Lord: I saw the Lord sitting on His throne, and all the host of heaven standing on His right hand and His left. And the Lord said, 'Who will persuade Ahab king of Israel to go up, that he may fall at Ramoth Gilead?' So one spoke in this manner, and another in that manner. Then a spirit came forward and stood before the Lord, and said, 'I will persuade him.' The Lord said to him, 'In what way?' So he said, **'I will go out and be a lying spirit in the mouth of all his prophets.' And the Lord said, 'You shall persuade him and also prevail; go out and do so.'" Therefore look! The Lord has put a lying spirit in the mouth of these prophets of yours, and the Lord has declared disaster against you** (2 Chr. 18:18-22).

The reason that the Lord will deceive those with idols in their heart is for their destruction, which is what happened to King Ahab. Ahab threw Micaiah into prison for his prophesy, went to battle with Jehoshaphat, and was killed in battle, but Jehoshaphat returned safely home. I believe his life was spared because he sought the truth. Balaam had an idol of greed in his heart, and God answered him according to that idol.

> Then the LORD put a word in Balaam's mouth, and said, "Return to Balak, and thus you shall speak." So he returned to him, and there he was, standing by his burnt offering, he and all the princes of Moab. And he took up his oracle and said: "Balak the king of Moab has brought me from Aram, from the mountains of the east. 'Come, curse Jacob for me, and come, denounce Israel!'" "How shall I curse whom God has not cursed? And how shall I denounce *whom* the LORD has not denounced? For from the top of the rocks I see him, and from the hills I behold him; There! A people dwelling alone, not reckoning

itself among the nations. "Who can count the dust of
Jacob, or number one-fourth of Israel? Let me die the
death of the righteous, and let my end be like his!" Then
Balak said to Balaam, "What have you done to me? I
took you to curse my enemies, and look, you have
blessed *them* bountifully!" So he answered and said,
"Must I not take heed to speak what the LORD has put in
my mouth" (Nu. 23:5-12)?

Balak tried two more times to get Balaam to curse Israel, but each time a blessing was spoken infuriating Balak. God ended His blessing of Israel by cursing Moab and then prophesying of the coming Messiah.

I see Him, but not now; I behold Him, but not near; a
Star shall come out of Jacob; a Scepter shall rise out of
Israel, and batter the brow of Moab, and destroy all the
sons of tumult (Nu. 24:17).

Balaam returned home, but he wasn't done trying to get the diviner's fee. According to the second prophesy, Balaam couldn't curse Israel because God "has not observed iniquity in Jacob, nor has He seen wickedness in Israel. The Lord his God is with him, and the shout of a king is among them" (Nu. 23:21). Balaam devised a plan to cause Israel to stumble into sin.

Now Israel remained in Acacia Grove, and the people
began to **commit harlotry** with the women of Moab.
They invited the people to sacrifices of their gods, and
the people **ate and bowed down to their gods**. So Israel
was joined to Baal of Peor, and the anger of the Lord
was aroused against Israel (Nu. 25:1-3).

Look, these women caused the children of Israel,
**through the counsel of Balaam, to trespass against
the Lord in the incident of Peor,** and there was a
plague among the congregation of the Lord (Nu. 31:16).

The fall of Israel after the blessings that Balaam spoke over them is striking. God gave us a clue to understanding their fall by stating that "Israel remained in Acacia Grove." Acacia is a type of wood that is often symbolic of the flesh. It is a very hard wood, and it is difficult to work with. In order to walk with God successfully, we must crucify the flesh. Don't stay camped out in the "Flesh Grove" catering to the flesh's desires. Following after the flesh will kill you because the fallen nature dwells in the flesh. For example, let's say you like chocolate. Fine. Have a candy bar once or twice a week. That's balance. However, the flesh is never balanced. It will crave chocolate several times a day. And it will scream and whine until it gets what it wants. If you don't silence it by crucifying it, which is simply praying for God's grace to overcome and telling it to hush, you will begin eating sweets several times a week or even several times a day. Eventually, this will take a toll on your health, cause obesity, and could kill you. We must learn that the enemy will use sin in the camp to open the door to our destruction. Actually, he often doesn't need a door. He just needs a crack!

Balak didn't need to curse Israel and then defeat them in battle. Instead, Balaam's plan to cause Israel to sin resulted in a plague that killed twenty-four thousand Israelites. I don't doubt that Balaam did indeed receive a reward for causing the Israelites to commit idol worship. And remember how we learned that God allows idols to speak to a person's heart for his destruction? According to Numbers 31:8, the Israelites killed Balaam of Peor with the sword. And what weapon is used to combat false doctrine? The double-edged sword of the Spirit, which is the Word of God.

Revelation 2:14, it says that Balaam taught Balak how to put a **stumbling block** in front of the children of Israel. "Stumbling block" in the Greek always denotes enticement to conduct that can ruin the person in question.[6] The doctrine of Balaam seduces unstable Christians to worship idols and commit fornication. Remember that Balaam was a true prophet who erred because of greed. And here is another interesting tidbit. "Balaam" means not of the people or foreigner in the Hebrew.[7] You could translate "the doctrine of Balaam" as "the doctrine of the foreigner" or "doctrine of one who is not of the people." Peter wrote much about these false teachers and false prophets who are foreigners but look like Christians.

> But these, like natural brute beasts made to be caught and destroyed, speak evil of the things they do not understand, and will utterly perish in their own corruption, and will receive the wages of unrighteousness, as those who count it pleasure to carouse in the daytime. They are spots and blemishes, carousing in their own deceptions while they feast with you, having eyes full of adultery and that cannot cease from sin, **enticing unstable souls**. They have a heart trained in covetous practices, and are accursed children. **They have forsaken the right way and gone astray, following the way of Balaam** the son of Beor, who loved the wages of unrighteousness...For if, **after they have escaped the pollutions of the world through the knowledge of the Lord and Savior Jesus Christ, they are again entangled in them and overcome, the latter end is worse for them than the beginning** (2 Peter 2:12-15,20).

This was such a problem during the time of the early church that Jude decided to write about it instead of writing about salvation (Jude 3). If false teachers were a problem 2,000 years ago, how much more of a problem are they now? If we think that we do not have this problem today, we are deceived. There are still Balaams, Cains, and Korahs among us who are very good at acting the Christian part.

> "Woe to them! For they have gone in the way of Cain, **have run greedily in the error of Balaam for profit,** and perished in the rebellion of Korah. These are spots in your love feasts, while they feast with you without fear, serving only themselves. They are clouds without water, carried about by the winds; late autumn trees without fruit, **twice dead,** pulled up by the roots; raging waves of the sea, foaming up their own shame; wandering stars for whom is reserved the blackness of darkness forever" (Jude 11-13).

The only way you can be "twice dead" is to be dead once, born again, and dead again. These Christians have gone astray for greed, and like Satan, are not happy going down by themselves but desire to take others with them. These search for unstable souls that are not yet rooted in the love of Christ and His Word.

Repent

> Repent, or else I will come to you quickly and will fight against them with the sword of My mouth (Rev. 2:16).

The Christians at Pergamos were instructed to repent. They needed to remove those who held to these false doctrines. As a holy body, we cannot tolerate those who knowingly teach or follow false doctrine and entice Christians into sexual sin and idolatry. Today idolatry isn't so much the worship of graven images but is instead the worship of money, self, position, religion, or anything that usurps God's rightful place. Christ warned the church at Pergamos that if they did not repent, He would quickly come to them and fight against them with the sword of His mouth. The very thing that was their weapon against false doctrine (the Word) would fight against them if they didn't repent.

> And He has made **My mouth like a sharp sword**; in the shadow of His hand He has hidden Me, and made Me a polished shaft; in His quiver He has hidden Me (Isa. 49:2).

> Therefore I have hewn them by the prophets, **I have slain them by the words of My mouth**; and your judgments are like light that goes forth (Hos. 6:5).

> And the lawless one will be revealed, whom **the Lord will consume with the breath of His mouth** and destroy with the brightness of His coming (2 Thess. 2:8).

> But with righteousness He shall judge the poor, and decide with equity for the meek of the earth; **He shall strike the earth with the rod of His mouth, and with the breath of His lips He shall slay the wicked** (Isa. 11:4).

> **Now out of His mouth goes a sharp sword, that with it He should strike the nations.** And He Himself will rule them with a rod of iron. He Himself treads the winepress of the fierceness and wrath of Almighty God (Rev. 19:15).

The Word cleanses us and sets us free, but it also judges us. When Jesus returns a second time, it will be for judgment and that judgment will be His Word. The beast or antichrist will come with false signs and wonders and with a false doctrine that the antichrist is god. And Christ will defeat Him with the Truth. As stated before, the only weapon against false doctrine is the Word. It is better to allow His Word to cleanse us and renew our minds now so that we know the will of God than to dismiss the Word and later be judged by it.

> The coming of the lawless one is according to the working of Satan, with all power, signs, and lying wonders, and with all unrighteous deception among those who perish, because **they did not receive a love of the truth, that they might be saved. And for this reason God will send them strong delusion, that they should believe the lie,** that they all may be condemned who did not believe the truth but had pleasure in unrighteousness (2 Thess. 2:9-12).

THE PROMISE

> He who has an ear, let him hear what the Spirit says to the churches. To him who overcomes I will give some of the hidden manna to eat. And I will give him a white stone, and on the white stone a new name written which no one knows except him who receives it (Revelation 2:17).

To understand the concept of the hidden manna, we must go back to where manna was first introduced. In Exodus 16, the Israelites journeyed from Elim to the Wilderness of Sin. At this point, they began to complain about the lack of meat and bread. In response to their complaints, God promised to send them "bread from heaven."

> And the children of Israel said to them, "Oh, that we had died by the hand of the Lord in the land of Egypt, when we sat by the pots of meat and when we ate bread to the full! For you have brought us out into this wilderness to kill this whole assembly with hunger." Then the Lord said to Moses, "Behold, I will rain bread from heaven for you. And the people shall go out and gather a certain quota every day, that I may test them, whether they will walk in My law or not" (Ex. 16:3,4).

Quickly, I want to point out a human tendency. The Israelites stated that when they were in Egypt, they sat by "pots of meat" and "ate bread to the full." However, as slaves, they did not sit by pots of meat or eat bread to the full. They lived a life of hardship but often during times of testing, we tend to view our past through "rose-colored glasses." We forget how miserable we were and begin to desire things of the past.

The next morning when the dew lifted, manna was left behind. The Israelites did not know what to call this bread so they named it manna, which means "whatness." Each Israelite gathered enough for his needs—no more, no less. Those who tried to store extra manna were surprised when it turned to worms overnight. Thankfully, today we have the scriptures to explain the manna and its importance to us, which the Israelites did not have.

> And you shall remember that the Lord your God led you all the way these forty years in the wilderness, to humble you and test you, to know what was in your heart, whether you would keep His commandments or not. So **He humbled you, allowed you to hunger,** and fed you with manna which you did not know nor did your fathers know, **that He might make you know that man does not live by bread alone; but man lives by every word that proceeds from the mouth of God** (Deut. 8:2,3).

Jesus As The Manna

> Then Jesus being filled with the Holy Spirit, returned from the Jordan and was **led by the Spirit into the**

> **wilderness**, being tempted for **forty** days by the devil.
> And in those days He ate nothing, and afterward, when
> they had ended, **He was hungry** (Luke 4:1,2).

Notice that *the Spirit* led Jesus into the wilderness. The length of temptation, 40 days, was a type of similar testing that the Israelites went through in the wilderness for 40 years. And like the Israelites, Jesus experienced hunger.

> And the devil said to Him, "If You are the Son of God,
> command this stone to become bread." But Jesus
> answered him, saying, "It is written, 'Man shall not live
> by bread alone, but by every word of God'" (Luke 4:3,4).

Jesus defeated the devil's temptation to use His power to produce bread by quoting the exact words God spoke to the Israelites in Deut. 8:3. In this passage, the Greek word *rhema* is used for word. *Rhema* means an utterance.[8] Jesus' reply could be translated, "Man shall not live by bread alone, but by every utterance of God." *Rhema* is in contrast to another Greek word used for "word" in the Bible, *logos*. *Logos* means something said, but more specifically it means the "Divine Expression," which found its place in Jesus Christ.[9] According to John 1:1, Jesus as the Word (*logos*) was in the beginning, was with God, and was God. Both imply spoken word, but rhema is a little different in that it is often used for personal utterances spoken to each of us individually. *Logos* is more of the Word as a whole, which includes the written Word but also Christ as a Person. Both are extremely important, and if you think about it, the Bible was at one point spoken by the Holy Spirit (*rhema*) into the hearts of men who were obedient to write it down. Therefore, I believe that when Jesus said we cannot live by bread alone but by every word of God, He meant the spoken words that are whispered in our spirits each day and our personal study or "eating" of the written Word, the Bible. We, like the Israelites, are to gather a certain quota of God's words, whether written or spoken, each day, and we cannot depend on yesterday's gathering to feed us today.

The "manna test" as I like to call it was also given to the disciples of Jesus. The day after the feeding of the five thousand (John

6:1-14), those same disciples went looking for Jesus. They found Him on the other side of the sea and asked Him when He got there.

> Jesus answered them and said, "Most assuredly, I say to you, **you seek Me, not because you saw the signs, but because you ate of the loaves and were filled.** Do not labor for the food which perishes, **but for the food, which endures to everlasting life, which the Son of Man will give you,** because God the Father has set His seal on Him" (John 6:26,27).

These disciples were being tested just as the Israelites were with the manna. Here, the people were seeking Jesus for more food to fill their stomachs. They didn't realize that the feeding of the five thousand was a sign that the True Bread from Heaven was in their midst (John 6:26).

> Then Jesus said to them, "Most assuredly, I say to you, Moses did not give you the bread from heaven, but My Father gives you the true bread from heaven. For the bread of God is He who comes down from heaven and gives life to the world"...And Jesus said to them, "**I am the bread of life. He who comes to Me shall never hunger,** and he who believes in Me shall never thirst. But I said to you that you have seen Me and yet do not believe...I am the bread of life. Your fathers ate the manna in the wilderness, and are dead. **This is the bread which comes down from heaven, that one may eat of it and not die. I am the living bread which came down from heaven. If anyone eats of this bread, he will live forever;** and the bread that I shall give is My flesh, which I shall give for the life of the world" (John 6:32,33,35,36,48-51).

If we eat of Him, we will have everlasting life. The manna from heaven in the wilderness was a prophecy of the coming Bread of Life. The disciples were as confused by what Jesus meant as the Israelites were about what the physical manna was.

Whoever eats My flesh and drinks My blood has eternal life, and I will raise him up at the last day...this is the bread which came down from heaven--not as your fathers ate the manna, and are dead. He who eats this bread will live forever...Therefore many of His disciples, when they heard this, said, "This is a hard saying; who can understand it?" When Jesus knew in Himself that His disciples complained about this, He said to them, "Does this offend you? What then if you should see the Son of Man ascend where He was before? It is the Spirit who gives life; the flesh profits nothing. The words that I speak to you are spirit, and they are life. But there are some of you who do not believe." For Jesus knew from the beginning who they were who did not believe, and who would betray Him...**From that time many of His disciples went back and walked with Him no more** (John 6:54, 58, 60-64,66).

Notice these are Jesus' disciples not the general population. They failed the "manna test" and quit following Him. Are we failing it also? Are we depending on others to eat His words for us and then tell us what He said? Do we go to church to be spoon-fed on Sunday and live on that for the rest of the week? Are our eyes more focused on God providing food, clothing, and other provision than on us living by His words? We need the other, but we must not forsake His words.

The hidden manna promised to those who overcome is life everlasting through Jesus Christ. And He is hidden. He must be sought after. Treasure is concealed or hidden. If you knew where an ancient pirate treasure worth millions was hidden, would you not forsake all to go get it? Jesus is the true treasure that only those who are willing to seek the kingdom first and leave provision in His care will find.

The White Stone

The second promise to those who overcome was a white stone with a new name written on it. In ancient times, juries voted for acquittal by casting a white stone into an urn. As believers, we have been acquitted of our sins. However, being born again isn't the end but the beginning. We must work out our salvation with fear and trembling (Phil. 2:12).

> Now if the righteous one is scarcely saved, where will the ungodly and the sinner appear (1 Pet. 4:18)?

"Scarcely" means with difficulty.[10] Crucifying the flesh, persecution, trials, and tribulations are difficulties, but Jesus said that we could rejoice because He has overcome the world and all its troubles (Jn. 16:33). Salvation is for those who endure until the end (Mt. 24:13). The words ungodly and sinner in the above scripture support this. Sinner is the unsaved. But ungodly is an interesting word and might not include just sinners. "Ungodly" means irreverent.[11] Irreverence is a lack of the fear of God. It is disrespect of Him and His ways. Do you know how many Christians do not truly fear Him? This is evident by the rampant sin in the church because the Bible says that the fear of God prevents us from sinning (Ex. 20:20). Things will change before the end. Many Christians will be confronted by God's power in a way that will restore a proper fear of Him. But we must not be deceived. God is not mocked. Whatever we sow, we will reap (Gal. 6:7-8). Many believe that receiving Christ is a guarantee of acquittal no matter how they live, but the Bible is clear that praying the sinner's prayer is not a guarantee (Matt. 7:21-23). The victorious end only comes when we endure and allow God to change us into His Son's image.

The white stone also carries an interesting meaning for those who dwelt in Pergamos. Remember the god Asklepios had a temple there. This god was represented by a serpent and was the god who healed sickness. The symbol of the serpent-entwined staff seen on the sides of ambulances is from this ancient worship of Asklepios. The "patient" would go to the temple at night and be given a substance to help him engage the god. Scholars believe it was some type of opiate. If the patient had a dream or vision of being healed, the priests would tell him it meant Asklepios healed them. Those who were healed would inscribe their sickness and name on white stones that lined the way into the temple as a testimony of their healing. Jesus no doubt had these stones in mind when He gave the promise of a white stone with a new name to those who overcome.

A New Name

"New" means not known before or newly introduced,[12] and "name" means title, character, reputation, and person.[13] Jacob was given a new name (Gen. 32:28). "Jacob" means usurper,[14] and God named him Israel, which means he will rule as God or prince of God.[15] This was a prophetic event of our future renaming. But God isn't going to stop at just giving us a new name. He is transforming us into Christ-likeness. Our spirits are transformed at our salvation, and the Word transforms our souls during our lifetime. And at the first resurrection, our bodies will be transformed like His (1 John 3:2). At this resurrection, we will be completely changed body, soul, and spirit into His character, reputation, and person!

One final thought on our new name. Among the Greeks and Romans, if a man did not have a son, he could adopt anyone including a slave as his son. The adoption process consisted of two parts: the private arrangement and the public declaration. In the private arrangement, the adopted son took the father's name and was regarded as his son in every aspect. He became the heir of his father's estate and no longer called his adopted father anything but abba. Spiritually, our private adoption is described in Romans 8:15, "For you did not receive the spirit of bondage again to fear, but you **received the Spirit of adoption by whom we cry out, 'Abba, Father.'"**

The public declaration proclaimed the adopted son as the legitimate son and heir of his new father to the world. Even if a slave, the adopted son was no longer regarded as a slave by the public. Spiritually, this public declaration is described in Romans 8:19,23, "For the earnest expectation of the creation eagerly waits for the revealing of the sons of God...Not only that, but we also who have the firstfruits of the Spirit, even we ourselves groan within ourselves, **eagerly waiting for the adoption, the redemption of our body.**" Our salvation is private, but our resurrection will be very public!

APPLICATION

The message to the church at Pergamos contains some practical insights that we, too, can implement in our lives. First, we must understand that we also live in the midst of "Satan's throne" (John 12:31). We are surrounded by idolatry in the world and in the church! And the enemy's plan is to make us friends with the world and its ways so that we are God's enemy (James 4:4) because he knows that opens us up to destruction. In order not to fall into his trap or stumbling block, we must live under God's authority and obey Him at all costs. We must keep ours hearts free from idolatry and covetousness and beware of false teachers and prophets. Remember, they look and act like Christians.

Second, in order to recognize false teachers, prophets, and doctrines, we must arm ourselves with the Word of God. Don't rely on your leaders to gather your manna for you and feed it to you once a week on Sunday. You will spiritually starve to death. Also, don't rely solely on your leaders for protection against false doctrine and prophecy. They are human and make mistakes. We all have the Holy Spirit and can discern truth from deception. Pray for your leaders and be watchful.

Those of you who are leaders must teach the Word in meekness, purity, and love. Guard your heart against cold love, hardness, greed, and rebellion. Identify all spots and wrinkles in your midst. Then ask the Holy Spirit for a divine, strategic plan for exposing and removing these, which will include repentance if you have allowed them to continue influencing any in your congregation. Ask for discernment to recognize the difference between a young Christian learning to operate his teaching or prophetic gift and a false teacher or prophet. A teacher or prophet that is immature will make mistakes but that does not label him as false. Peter made the biggest mistakes of any of the apostles, but he also had some of the greatest victories. He wasn't afraid to start over when he fell, and the grace was there for him to do so.

5 THYATIRA

And to the angel of the church in Thyatira write...
(Revelation 2:18)

Thyatira was a city in the northern part of Lydia, which was a Roman province of Asia. Thyatira was not on any significant trade routes, but instead was located on the lesser road between Pergamos and Sardis. Even though Thyatira was of lesser significance than the cities of the other churches in Revelation, it was a wealthy city and was especially known for its numerous guilds each with its own deity and for the purple dye it produced. The cloth dyed there had a reputation for being unsurpassed for its brilliance and permeance of color (Acts 16:14).

What is significant about Thyatira is that of all the churches in Revelation the meaning of its name is unknown. Today, Thyatira is called Ashisar, which means white castle.[1] The lack of a known meaning for Thyatira and the meaning of its modern name are important and relate to the message and promise given by Christ, which we'll discuss later in this chapter.

EXORTATION

These things says the Son of God, who has eyes like a flame of fire, and His feet like fine brass (Revelation 2:18b).

In addressing Thyatira, Jesus first called Himself the Son of God establishing His unique relationship as God's only Son. Next, the Lord provided two descriptive characteristics of Himself—eyes like fire and feet like fine brass. Let's examine both of these descriptions and unveil their mysteries.

First, His eyes of fire. In the Bible, fire often represents zeal and holiness. The Bible speaks of the refining fire often in conjunction with purifying fine metals especially gold. The gold and the refining process represent our relationship with the Lord. When purifying gold, the flame must be constantly maintained at a specific temperature. The refiner watches the process closely. As impurities rise to the surface, he ladles them off. This process is repeated until the refiner sees his reflection in the gold. Once this is reached, the gold is in its purist form.

The same is true for our walk. The Lord uses the fire of trials, persecutions, and tribulations to bring the impurities in our hearts to the surface. That was the purpose of the Israelites going through the wilderness. God was trying to remove Egypt from their souls. Only the Lord knows the perfect temperature and length of time that will produce His reflection in us.

When gold is in its purest form, it is very soft. For this reason, most jewelry is a combination of different metals, called an alloy that hardens the gold preventing damage. I remember I could put indents into my 24-caret gold class ring simply by pressing my fingernail into the gold. Being tender before the Lord can make us more susceptible to hurts and disappointments, but the Lord doesn't want us hardened by any other "metals." He wants us completely pliable in His hands and to see His reflection in us and uses those hurts and disappointments to refine us if we allow Him.

> For no other foundation can anyone lay than that which is laid, which is Jesus Christ. Now if anyone builds on this foundation with gold, silver, precious stones, wood, hay, straw, each one's work will become clear, **for the Day will declare it, because it will be revealed by fire; and the fire will test each one's work of what sort it is.** If anyone's work which he has built on it endures, he

will receive a reward. If anyone's work is burned, he will suffer loss; but he himself will be saved, yet so as through fire (1 Cor. 3:11-15).

"Day" is often used to describe the second coming. In this coming, the Lord will return as a consuming fire (Heb. 12:29). This is totally different from His first coming. When He first graced our planet, He came as a Lamb to redeem others to Himself. In the second coming, He will return as a Lion to bring justice. If He had come as fire at the first coming, everything would have been destroyed without redemption. Even so, His second coming isn't the act of a hateful God gleefully destroying everything in His path. No, it is a picture of a God who lovingly gave man 2,000 years to accept His Son's free gift of salvation. For those who did accept His gift, it will be a day of joy, and for those who did not, it will be a day of wrath (2 Thess. 1:8). Regardless, the Lord must set things straight on this earth at His return. He cannot let man continue forever destroying His creation and each other. We can be assured that His judgments are pure and right.

> The fear of the Lord is clean, enduring forever; the judgments of the Lord are true and righteous altogether (Ps. 19:9).

The next descriptive characteristic of the Lord was feet of fine brass. Feet and brass both speak of His stability, permanence, immovability, and omnipotence (all power). Brass is a mixture of copper and zinc and was considered the most durable of all metals, but it is probable that the brass spoken of here was not a simple brass. Fine brass is the Greek word *chalkolibano* and only occurs in Revelation 1:15 and 2:18. It literally means "white brass" and was probably a type of brass that was distinguished for its whiteness.[2] One such highly prized brass mixture was made of gold and brass. Another mixture valued for its brilliancy was made of four parts gold and one part silver. Gold speaks of His divinity, and silver speaks of redemption. A final mixture was copper melted with lapis calaminaris. The melting process occurred in underground furnaces. The flame that burned during this process was painfully vivid and bright. Could this be the picture John had in mind when he wrote, "His feet were like fine brass, as if refined in a furnace"

(Rev. 1:15a)?

Even though it's impossible to know what mixture John had in mind, we can surmise by the fire and fine brass that a refining was coming to the church at Thyatira. As you will see, Thyatira was corrupt. They had allowed a Jezebel to have a place of authority in their church. And the Lord wanted to let them know where He stood. He was not moving on this matter (feet of brass), and He wanted to purify this church (fire). But brass also has another meaning in scripture—judgment against sins of disobedience. As you will see, the Lord gave a specific warning if Jezebel wasn't properly dealt with.

> I know your works, love, service, faith, and your
> patience; and as for your works, the last are more than
> the first (Rev. 2:19).

Jezebel

Christ told the Christians at Thyatira that their latter works were more than their beginning works. This is in contrast to the message given to the church at Ephesus, which was rebuked for continuing with works but leaving their first love. It seems that Thyatira continued the first work of love while also pursuing other works of righteousness (Jms. 2:17-24).

> Nevertheless I have a few things against you, because **you allow** that woman Jezebel, who calls herself a prophetess, to teach and seduce My servants to commit sexual immorality and eat things sacrificed to idols (Rev. 2:20).

To understand what was going on at Thyatira and to avoid the same mistake, let's closely examine this verse. First, Jesus said that they allowed Jezebel a place of "ministry," teaching and seducing. "Allow" is the Greek word *eao*, which means, "to *let be*, that is, *permit* or *leave alone*:—commit, leave, let (alone), suffer."[3] One definition that stands out to me is "to leave alone." A problem will not simply disappear if we ignore it, and most of the problems in the church are in dealing with people. Even so, Christians tend to not confront issues because the Scriptures command us to pursue peace with all men (Heb. 12:14);

therefore, we mistakenly believe that confronting issues is not pursuing peace. However, Proverbs 27:5 says, "Open rebuke is better than carefully concealed love." Is it love to allow someone to continue ministering deception leading God's children astray? Is it love to allow a friend to continue down the wrong path without lovingly rebuking them? Is it love to allow our children to misbehave because we don't want to disrupt the peace? By ignoring the problem, the church leadership at Thyatira gave Jezebel authority by default. If you do not properly exercise the authority God has given you, you are in essence handing that authority to the enemy to use for his purposes.

"Woman" in this verse is *gune*, and it means woman but specifically a wife.[4] It is interesting to note that a majority of Greek Bible texts read "your wife Jezebel" instead of "that woman Jezebel." I believe we have lost some of the meaning of what Jesus was saying by translating this phrase as "that woman Jezebel." In order to understand where the Lord was coming from, we need to go back into Israelite history when the real Jezebel "ruled."

> In the thirty-eighth year of Asa king of Judah, Ahab the son of Omri became king over Israel; and Ahab the son of Omri reigned over Israel in Samaria for twenty-two years. Now Ahab the son of Omri did evil in the sight of the Lord, more than all who were before him. And it came to pass, as though it had been a trivial thing for him to walk in the sins of Jeroboam the son of Nebat, **that he took as wife Jezebel** the daughter of Ethbaal, king of the Sidonians; **and he went and served Baal and worshiped him.** He set up an altar for Baal in the temple of Baal, which he built in Samaria. And Ahab made a wooden image. **Ahab did more to provoke the Lord God of Israel to anger than all the kings of Israel who were before him** (1 Kings 16:29-33).

During this time, Israel and Judah were divided kingdoms because Solomon had worshiped idols (1 Kings 11:11-13). His unfaithfulness resulted in his son only ruling two tribes, Judah and Benjamin. God gave the other ten tribes to Jeroboam, one of Solomon's former servants. However, Jeroboam was insecure in his role as king and afraid the people would return to Rehoboam; therefore, Jeroboam set up his own temple, priests, altar, and religion in Samaria, the capital of his kingdom. This was a false religion. The true worship of God could only be at His prescribed place and His way. Jeroboam's actions plummeted the children of Israel into idolatry. Later, King Ahab, who ruled over the ten tribes of Israel, accelerated the spiritual and moral decline of the people by his willful, blatant idolatry.

Ahab's wife Jezebel was an ardent worshiper of Baal employing over 400 of this god's prophets. According to 1 Kings 18:4, she massacred God's prophets, and she was a fierce enemy of Elijah. She had strong supernatural powers, which is evident in that one threat from her mouth sent Elijah into a depression and brought about a premature end of his ministry. This was after he had killed her 400 prophets of Baal (1 King 19-1-18). She stirred Ahab to wickedness (1 Kings 21:25), and she used witchcraft (2 Kings 9:22). She was a strong woman who ruled Israel "behind-the-scenes" while leading her weak-willed husband to believe he was the one in authority over Israel (1 Kings 21:7). This unnatural relationship between Jezebel and Ahab was not according to God's order (Gen. 3:16b & Eph. 5:22). Because Ahab, as king of Israel, allowed Jezebel to be "lord" in this marriage, she was in reality the authority of Israel. He did not properly exercise the authority given him, so the enemy used that authority through Jezebel to lead Israel into more self-destructive behavior. This reveals an important principle—a leader is only a leader if he has followers (Prov. 14:28), and wherever the leader goes, the followers go.

Today, this spirit that operated in Jezebel still seeks to marry herself to God's people, which is the church. This spirit seeks influence and authority in marriages, churches, and even the government. That is why the Lord used a Greek word for woman that could also mean wife. He was revealing how this spirit operates.

This spirit, often called a Jezebel spirit because she personified this evil influence, has been around since the beginning, and I believe played a major role in the fall of man. Remember that this spirit often works through women especially wives. In Genesis 3:17, God rebuked

Adam for heeding the voice of his wife instead of His voice, which is a major characteristic of husbands that are married to women under this spirit's influence. Women must be aware of the influence they have over others especially their families, and men must dwell with their wives in understanding but not to the point of disobedience to God's clear direction. And, of course, the same is true for women, but a wife must always have a submissive spirit even if she can't obey her husband because his request is violating clear Scripture.

I believe women with strong personalities are more prone to this spirit's influence. I have a strong personality and had a Jezebel spirit for years. I was controlling, hard, and manipulative (manipulation is witchcraft). Fortunately, God did not give me a weak, passive, and lazy husband. Instead, my husband had a will of iron and refused to be controlled by this spirit, which greatly helped in exposing its influence in my life and led to my eventual deliverance. However, it should be said that any woman and even men can be under this spirit's influence.

A woman with this spirit might struggle in remaining faithful to her husband. She also has trouble trusting or waiting upon God, so she manipulates circumstances and people to get her way. I frequently used my "powers of manipulation" to get what I wanted. I remember one time I needed an office chair. My father-in-law had one and in my mind he wasn't using it. I proceeded to tell him how I needed a chair just like his, and within a few minutes, he gave me his. I realize now that a demonic spirit gave power to my words and influenced others to do what I wanted. After God revealed this to me, I had to learn to trust Him for my needs. I can't tell you how many times I was tempted to resort to the old, manipulative ways. Now, I am free from this spirit's influence. It took a lot of hard work and obedience, but anyone who has this spirit can be free through the grace of God.

Jezebel's influence in the church is often directed toward a pastor in order to gain a place of authority or can influence a leader's wife so that she rules "behind-the-scenes." She is usually fiercely protective of her husband, but this is only a tactic of this spirit to protect its position. If the Jezebel is in a woman, it might use the woman to seduce the pastor. If successful, it then sets about causing a divorce, so it can gain influence in the church by arranging for the woman to marry the pastor and exert authority through him. If this is unsuccessful, this spirit will use slander to destroy the uncooperative pastor. Jezebel causes division and church splits. This spirit might also be found in home groups sowing seeds of division. If it is not stopped, it will seduce and lead many astray and destroy ministries. This spirit is powerful and must not be underestimated. Even so, He who is in us is greater than this spirit (1 John 4:4).

Personally, each time I have confronted this spirit, I have not come away unscathed. An example that comes to mind occurred years ago with my husband's job. God had shown me that two gentlemen would take over the business he worked at. Two years later, two men desired to buy the business and began negotiations; however, every time a deal was agreed upon between my husband's boss and these two men, it would fall apart. I began to notice that it always happened after my husband's boss went home and came back the next day. I had discerned earlier that his wife might have a Jezebel spirit so I decided to pray about it. God instructed me to go against the Jezebel spirit in this woman only to the degree that she was manipulating the business deal. A week later, the deal was finalized.

Afterward I felt heaviness in the form of sadness for several days. God revealed to me in prayer that I was attacked with heaviness because I went against a Jezebel spirit. I remembered that this was what happened to Elijah hundreds of years ago. I went against the heaviness and immediately felt better. Since that time, I am able to recognize her attacks quicker, and I am able to minister to others who are also attacked by her and do not realize it.

We can learn many things from the story of Jezebel especially how NOT to be a Jezebel! I recommend all wives to study her story and any who feel a prophetic call because the enemy will try to turn the prophetically gifted into Jezebels. We do not know if the woman Jezebel that was in Thyatira started out as a person with a legitimate prophetic gift. But by calling herself a prophetess, we can ascertain that she felt labels were important. True prophets will not go around calling themselves anything. They let the people label them. Of course, the immature may for a while, but we must discern the immature from the false. Also, like the prophet Balaam who became false, this woman taught the people to commit spiritual and physical adultery, which is definitely a sign of a false prophet. God instructs us not to listen or obey a "prophet" who prophesies even with signs and wonders and then tells us to go after other gods (Deut. 13:2).

With the understanding of Jezebel, let's get back to the original question as to why Jesus said "your wife Jezebel" in verse 20. The person Jezebel was married to was the king of Israel. Israel was a shadow of the future spiritual Israel, which is the church (Acts 7:38). The spirit of Jezebel still seeks to marry the church. Satan knows that if a church tolerates the spirit of Jezebel and gives her authority even by simply leaving her alone, he can plunge that church into idolatry and deception eventually destroying it.

> And I gave her time to repent of her sexual immorality, and she did not repent. Indeed I will cast her into a sickbed, and those who commit adultery with her into great tribulation, unless they repent of their deeds. I will kill her children with death, and all the churches shall know that I am He who searches the minds and hearts. And I will give to each one of you according to your works (Rev. 3:21-23).

Jesus then clearly stated the consequences of Jezebel's actions and any who followed her. He first showed His mercy in allowing her time to repent, which she refused. The word "time" used in this verse denotes the passing of moments.[5] It reminds me of a clock—tick, tock—and time passing by. "Repent" is to change one's mind for the better, and heartily to amend with abhorrence of one's past sins.[6] Now her punishment is a sickbed. This goes against much theology in the western church today. Many feel that they can continue to live the lives they desire along with the sin they commit and not get in trouble. However, God warns us that He is not mocked, and we reap what we sow. If we sow to the flesh (its deeds), we will reap corruption (Gal. 6:7,8). Corruption means decay and ruin. Jude warns us of those "who turn the grace of our God into lewdness and deny the only Lord God and our

Lord Jesus Christ" (Jude 1:4). How do these deny Him? By their actions. Grace is not the excuse to continue living as we did before we got saved. Grace is the working of the Holy Spirit on our hearts that results in change that is reflected in our outward lives. Grace enables us to serve Him acceptably. We must realize that if we have unrepentant sin in our lives, we can fall into sickness, poverty, and many more unpleasant situations that are not God's will for our lives.

This reminds me of a Christian woman I knew. One day I received a phone call that she was dead! You can imagine my surprise that a middle-aged woman in good health was dead. Her son had found her barely breathing one morning. At first, they thought that she had choked on a bite of pizza. Later, it was determined that her organs had shut down due to a long history of prescription drug abuse. She sowed to her flesh, and her flesh (body) died. The wages of sin is death (Rom. 6:23). A Christian is not immune to the consequences of rebellion.

Those that committed adultery with Jezebel were warned of great tribulation if they did not repent. They, too, had time to change their minds. "Great tribulation" is anguish, affliction, and trouble.[7] Christ also stated that He would kill her children. Who were Jezebel's children? *Thayer's Greek Definitions* states that "in the NT, pupils or disciples are called children of their teachers, because the latter by their instruction nourish the minds of their pupils and mould their characters."[8] Remember that Jezebel was teaching others (Rev. 2:20). She had disciples that she was molding into her image. These had to be removed or the sin would spread. King Ahab and Jezebel's children were killed as well (2 Kings 10).

> You shall strike down the house of Ahab your master,
> that I may avenge the blood of My servants the prophets,
> and the blood of all the servants of the Lord, at the hand
> of Jezebel. For the whole house of Ahab shall perish;
> and I will cut off from Ahab all the males in Israel, both
> bond and free (2 Kings 9:7,8).

"All the churches shall know that I am He who searches the minds and hearts. And I will give to each of you according to your works," declared Jesus (Rev. 2:23). We should not dismiss these words.

Having a healthy fear of the Lord is to our benefit. Exodus 20:20 tells us that a godly fear will prevent us from sinning. The enemy has done two things in our day to prevent a healthy fear of God. He has perverted this fear into terror, which causes Christians to believe that God is up in heaven on His throne eagerly looking for anyone who messes up so He can squash them like a bug. However, Scripture declares that He is slow to anger and that His eyes run to and fro throughout the earth to show Himself strong on behalf of those who are loyal to Him (2 Chr. 16:9). The second tactic of the enemy has been to deceive people into thinking they are getting away with sin, which is the exact opposite of the first tactic.

> Because the sentence against an evil work is not executed speedily, therefore the heart of the sons of men is fully set in them to do evil. Though a sinner does evil a hundred *times,* and his *days* are prolonged, yet I surely know that it will be well with those who fear God, who fear before Him (Eccl. 8:11, 12).

People believe the enemy's lie that they will not reap what they sow. In the garden, Eve added to God's words and said that she couldn't even touch the fruit of the tree of knowledge of good and evil (Gen. 3:3). Satan used her misunderstanding to deceive her. I'm sure when she touched the tree and did not die that this made the enemy's lies even more believable. People "touch" sin and nothing happens. Then they begin to "eat" sin's fruit and nothing happens. They lose fear of the Lord. They go deeper and deeper into darkness so that when consequences do begin to manifest, they blame others for their problems instead of accepting responsibility. We must be careful to know God's Word for in it is the keys to understanding Him and His character. Then we must obey the Word so we are not deceived (Jms. 1:22).

As Christians, we must understand that the path of life has ditches on either side—lawlessness or legalism. We must balance the fear of the Lord (Lion of Judah) and the love of the Lord (the Lamb) so that we do not become religious or use His grace as an excuse to continue in sin (Rom. 11:22). It is a sign of maturity to walk in this balance.

> Now to you I say, and to the rest in Thyatira, as many as do not have this doctrine, who have not known the depths of Satan, as they say, I will put on you no other burden. But hold fast what you have till I come (Rev. 2:24,25).

A final thought before we go onto the promises He gave Thyatira. He told those at Thyatira to hold fast what they had until He came. Obviously, the people of this ancient church have died and He hasn't come yet. This is one more reason I believe the messages to each church in the book of Revelation are as important for us to understand as it was for them. These were meant for all believers throughout the centuries but especially for those of us alive at this last hour.

THE PROMISE

> And he who overcomes, and keeps My works until the end, to him I will give power over the nations—"He shall rule them with a rod of iron; they shall be dashed to pieces like the potter's vessels"—as I also have received from My Father (Rev. 2:26,27).

Remember that God told me that each church's name in Revelation matched the message the Lord gave them. What is interesting about Thyatira is that Thyatira is of uncertain meaning in the Greek. We could say it is a no-name city compared to the other churches that had specific meanings. We must also remember that Thyatira was of lesser significance than the other cities that received messages; therefore, it was a no-name, insignificant city. Yet, the first promise that Jesus makes to this less significant city is "I will give [you] power over the nations," the same power that Christ received from His Father. The word "power" is *exousia. Thayer's Greek Definitions* lists numerous meanings including "the power of authority (influence) and of right (privilege), the power of rule or government (the power of him whose will and commands must be submitted to by others and obeyed), one who possesses authority, the sign of regal authority, a crown." [9]

Simply put, we could translate His promise as, "I will give [you] authority over the nations." As stated, its modern day name means "white castle." When we think of castles, we picture kings and queens ruling from them. This is just like God. He takes the insignificant, the rejected, and the forgotten and makes it great. Even so, we must understand that if we are to rule the nations along side Him, we, too, must overcome any Jezebel tendencies in ourselves, churches, and marriages. You know what makes this promise so exciting to me? It is not so much the thought of ruling but the thought that because we rule, we will have more contact with the King. To me, the most contact and fellowship I can get with Him in heaven, the better.

And I will give him the morning star (Rev. 2:28).

Understanding this promise required quite a bit of digging. But it is the glory of God to conceal things and our glory to search them out (Prov. 25:2). To understand what the morning star is, let's go to 2 Peter 1:16-19.

> For we do not follow cunningly devised fables when we made known to you the power and coming of our Lord Jesus Christ, but were eyewitnesses of His majesty. For He received from God the Father honor and glory when such a voice came to Him from the Excellent Glory: "This is My beloved Son, in whom I am well pleased." And we heard this voice which came from heaven when we were with Him on the holy mountain. And so we have the prophetic word confirmed, which you do well to heed as a light that shines in a dark place, until the day dawns and the morning star rises in your hearts.

What on earth is Peter talking about? First, let's look at the word "coming" in the above passage. "Coming" is the Greek word *parousia*. *Parousia* is only used to describe the second coming NOT the first coming.[10] Yet, Peter is saying that they made known to us the power and *parousia* of Jesus and that they were eyewitnesses! How can this be since He has not returned for the second time? The rest of the passage gives us some clues.

Peter next described a voice from heaven saying, "This is My beloved Son, in whom I am well pleased." Some say this is speaking of

Jesus' baptism. But Peter stated that he was an eyewitness, but Peter wasn't at Jesus' baptism. He wasn't even chosen as an apostle yet. Also, Peter says specifically that he and the others **heard** this voice. They not only saw His glory and majesty, but they heard the Father speak to them about the Son. Peter also says this event occurred on a mountain, which also rules out Jesus' baptism because He was baptized in a river not on a mountain. From these clues, I believe we can conclude that Peter is talking about one of the most mysterious events in the Word—the transfiguration. Let's investigate and see if it fits the hypothesis. First, we need to look at what Jesus said right before the transfiguration.

> Then Jesus said to His disciples, "If anyone desires to come after Me, let him deny himself, take up his cross, and follow Me. For whoever desires to save his life will lose it, but whoever loses his life for My sake will find it. For what profit is it to a man if he gains the whole world, and loses his own soul? Or what will a man give in exchange for his soul? For the Son of Man will come in the glory of His Father with His angels, and then He will reward each according to his works. Assuredly, I say to you, **there are some standing here who shall not taste death till they see the Son of Man coming in His kingdom** (Matt. 16:24-28)."

Disciple means learner or student.[11] Jesus was speaking to His students not the multitudes. He was conveying to them the secret of entering His kingdom, which is denying oneself and daily taking up the cross to follow Him. Taking up our cross is simply obeying Him even to the point of putting to death our own will, agenda, and desires. He then promised that He is coming back in His glory with His angels and will reward all of us according to our works. Remember, He told the church at Thyatira the same thing (Rev. 2:23). And then He said a strange thing, "There are some standing here who shall not taste death till they see the Son of Man coming in His kingdom." Keep this statement in mind as you read the next passage.

> Now after six days Jesus took Peter, James, and John his brother, led them up on a high **mountain** by themselves;

and He was transfigured before them. His face shone like the sun, and His clothes became as white as the light. And behold, Moses and Elijah appeared to them, talking with Him. Then Peter answered and said to Jesus, "Lord, it is good for us to be here; if you wish, let us make here three tabernacles: one for You, one for Moses, and one for Elijah." While he was still speaking, behold, a bright cloud overshadowed them; and suddenly a voice came out of the cloud, saying, "**This is My beloved Son, in whom I am well pleased. Hear Him** (Matt. 17:1-5)!"

Jesus told them that some *standing there* would not die until they saw Him come into His kingdom. Those "standing there" are those He was instructing on taking up their cross and following Him. Now we know that after 2,000 years, not one of His disciples are alive and on this earth today, so Jesus had to mean something other than His literal second coming. I believe scripture is clear that event was His transfiguration, which matches the clues that we got from 2 Peter. 1:16-19. Peter, James, and John were eyewitnesses. This event occurred on a mountain, and a voice spoke from heaven the exact thing Peter told us.

But why did Peter use the word *parousia* to describe the transfiguration if *parousia* only speaks of His second coming? I believe he used *parousia* because the transfiguration is a prophetic picture of His second coming. For example, it is significant that Jesus took them up the mountain after six days, which means the transfiguration happened on the seventh day. Remember that a day is as a thousand years, and a thousand years is as a day (2 Peter 3:8). God made the earth in six days and rested on the seventh. Jesus said He is Lord of the Sabbath (Mark 2:28). His second coming will be on the seventh day from the creation of mankind,[12] and it will usher in the millennial reign, which will be a 1,000 years of rest (Sabbath) from Satan because he will be bound. Also, Jesus was raised from the dead on the third day. He was here 2,000 years ago or two days ago. We are going into the third day since His first coming.

> After **two days** He will revive us; on the **third day He will raise us up**, that we may live in His sight (Hosea 6:2).

The catching away involves the raising of the dead all who sleep in Christ (1 Thess. 4:15-17). Just as Christ was raised on the third day so also will the dead in Christ and those who are alive be resurrected.

And, finally, we need to notice that Matthew 17:2 says, "His face shone like the sun." The sun is a star that rises every morning in the east. Only in the book of Revelation does Jesus call Himself a star (Rev. 2:28 & 22:16). Second Peter 1:19 tells us that the "prophetic word" of Jesus' second coming was confirmed by the transfiguration, and we are cautioned to heed this prophetic word until "the day dawns and the morning star rises in our hearts." Jesus is the Morning Star.

> "For behold, the day is coming, burning like an oven, and all the proud, yes, all who do wickedly will be stubble. And the day which is coming shall **burn** them up," says the Lord of hosts, "that will leave them neither root nor branch. But to you who fear My name the **Sun of Righteousness shall arise** with healing in His wings..." (Mal. 4:1,2).

APPLICATION

The message to the church at Thyatira touches upon one of the most important principles in God's kingdom: authority. God is King over a kingdom. That's it. It is not a democracy. Those of us who live in America tend to equate God's rule as a democracy. We must realize that God is authority, and He places individuals in authority that we are to submit to and obey. And it is possible to gain authority illegally like Jezebel did. As individuals, we must always be watchful for the tendency to be Jezebel because God placed in all of us the desire to rule. This occurred at the garden when He gave Adam and Eve authority over all the earth (Gen. 1:28). Since that authority has been lost, man has tried any way possible to gain it back apart from the cross.

The message to the Christians at Thyatira also reveals that the time for repentance does run out. Moments pass by and reaping what we've sowed begins to occur. We all have harvests in our lives. God said that as long as the earth remains there will be seedtime and harvest (Gen. 8:22). Notice seed + time = harvest. It is the time that gets us. We sow whether for life or corruption and nothing happens immediately. If we have sown to the flesh, we feel bolder in our sin because we weren't "struck by lightening." If we sow to the Spirit, we sometimes get frustrated when our circumstances don't change overnight. However, you can rest assured that the harvest will come.

And, finally, this message reveals that even if you seem insignificant in the scheme of things, you are not. Jesus told us that the last will be first and the first last (Matt. 20:16). He also said that the greatest in the kingdom is a servant to all (Matt. 23:11). In heaven, angels step aside in respect to those who grasped the servant's heart on this earth. If your life seems insignificant, ask the Lord for a revelation of what is significant to Him. You might be surprised by His answer because He will probably not tell you a worldwide ministry. It is simply loving others and going about doing good. In all of this, we must remember that we are here to love Him with every ounce of our being and love others as ourselves (Matt. 22:37), which is the most significant thing we can do on this earth.

6 SARDIS

> And to the angel of the church in Sardis write...
> (Revelation 3:1)

Sardis was the capital of Lydia, a country in Asia Minor. It was located about 50 miles northeast from Smyrna and thirty miles southeast of Thyatira. Sardis was situated at the base of Mount Tmolus on the river Pactolus, which was celebrated for its golden sands. The river Hermes, a site of great beauty, was located two miles away. Sardis was not only a place of beauty but also of wealth due to its convenience as a commercial market and its prosperous manufacturers. It is here that Croesus, a king whose name was synonymous with wealth, reigned. Croesus issued the first gold coins. In 548 B.C., Cyrus conquered Croesus and took his treasure. Over time, Sardis fell into the hands of several rulers including Alexander the Great. It was devastated by an earthquake in 17 A.D. but was rebuilt, which testifies to its continued wealth and importance.

The church at Sardis was corrupted by the city's prevailing worldliness, decadence, and luxury, which resulted in the sternest rebuke from the Lord. It is my supposition that Sardis, along with Laodicea, most represent the current condition of the western church. By western church, I am discussing the body of Christ that lives in the western hemisphere that includes North America and much of Europe. The western nations are mostly characterized by prosperity and democracy.

On the opposite side of the scale, the Eastern Church, including the Asian and Middle Eastern regions, is best characterized as the persecuted church. Persecution stems from its own governments and militant religious factions. Even though persecution, poverty, and oppression are characteristic of this region, some of the most amazing miracles and acts of God occur on a regular basis. Not only that, but the love and zeal for the Lord is often at its highest peak among the persecuted church while passivity and lawlessness abounds in the church where "freedom reigns." Even so, I once heard it said that persecution is not God's favored method to produce on- fire Christians. He would rather have us walk with Him in freedom instead of in persecution because He loves freedom, which is why Paul said to pray for our governments so that we can dwell in peace (1 Tim. 2:2).

Sadly, most Christians only cling to God when they are in trouble. Take away the trouble, and you are left with Christians who have forgotten God. However, God will have this testimony: He will have a people who are obedient and intimate with Him in the midst of a very imperfect environment. This is the highest glory God will receive for Adam and Eve disobeyed in the midst of a perfect environment, and its fulfillment will be the greatest vengeance against Satan other than the cross and resurrection of Jesus.

The message to Sardis is predominately a message to the western church; however, I am reluctant to lump all churches in the west together. Many churches in the west are on fire for the Lord. But I believe that the message to Sardis' church can help churches that are on fire for Him stay focused, and churches that are almost dead to resurrect. Because Jesus' message to Sardis was stern, this teaching may seem sterner than others. I pray that you hear the Spirit in this teaching tearing down *and* building up for He never tears down only; He always offers us hope and a future.

EXORTATION

These things says He who has the seven Spirits of God and the seven stars: "I know your works, that you have a name that you are alive, but you are dead" (Revelation 3:1b).

Christ began His message to Sardis by declaring that He possesses the seven Spirits of God and the seven stars. As discussed in the introduction, the number seven is a cardinal number that represents perfection and completion. The Holy Spirit is not seven different spirits but one; however, He is perfect and complete. Isaiah 11:1-2 lists the seven perfect characteristics of the Spirit of God—the Lord's rule, wisdom, understanding, counsel, might, knowledge, and fear of God. The same application applies to the seven stars. Remember that Revelation 1:20 says that the stars are the angels of the seven churches, and angel means messenger and by implication pastor in the Greek. He holds seven stars because this message (and all the messages) is to all pastors throughout church history and all future pastors. In other words, this message didn't die hundreds of years ago with the church at Sardis. God's Word is living and powerful (Heb. 4:12) and just as relevant today if not even more so.

> "I know your works, that you have a name that you are alive, but you are dead" (Rev. 3:1b).

In ancient cultures, a person's name was synonymous with his reputation. The same is true to an extent today. For example, if I say, President George W. Bush, your mind is immediately filled with descriptive words about President Bush such as honest, dishonest, godly, religious, wise, stupid, and more depending on whether your opinion of him is favorable or not. Our goal as Christians is to have a good name or reputation, which is "to be chosen rather than great riches (Prov. 22:1). We should be people who are known by our faithfulness, love, and righteousness. We should be known as people who do everything with excellence and keep our word. Sadly, the name *Christian* is often one of shame because we haven't lived up to the high calling of that name.

The impact of a name extends to many not just one. Using our same example of the name *Christian,* you may be a person of faithfulness, love, and righteousness, but you will be thought of according to the general estimate of Christians held by the public. If that estimation is unfavorable, you might be viewed unfavorably even though you live up to the name of Christian. The more public the name, the more impact it has on others as a whole. This is why God holds the value of a good name as more than great riches. He knows the power a name holds. Even so, the Bible says that Jesus made Himself of no reputation (Phil. 2:7). In other words, He emptied Himself of His privileges as God and veiled His deity in the form of human flesh so that faith was required to believe in Him as the Christ or Messiah. This tells me that we should not hold our reputation as more important than our obedience to God. Sometimes people will ridicule us because of our obedience. God uses these times as a test to see whether we fear Him or man more.

According to *Thayer's Greek Definitions*, "name" is "used for everything which the name covers, everything the thought or feeling of which is aroused in the mind by mentioning, hearing, remembering, the name, i.e. for one's rank, authority, interests, pleasure, command, excellencies, deeds etc."[1] Because of the importance of a name, great care was taken in naming a child. The ancient Hebrews linked a person's name with their character. Sometimes the child's name was descriptive of the parents' dreams for their child. Other times a child was named based on the condition of their country and society. The importance of a child's name stems from God's heart for names. He named and renamed individuals several times in the Bible. Abram was changed to Abraham. Sarai was changed to Sarah. Jacob was changed to Israel. He told Mary to name her unborn child Jesus. Jesus renamed Simon by giving him the name Peter. All of these names carried significant meanings or showed a change in character. Jesus means "Salvation," which the Lord brought to us. Simon meant unstable, and Peter meant rock, which spoke of Peter's future stability. Jacob, which meant deceiver, was renamed Israel, which meant "Prince of God." Names were also prophetic. Every time Abraham's name was spoken, his future as a father to many nations was being prophesied.

God uses various names to reveal His character and attributes. For example, Jehovah-Jireh means "The Lord Will Provide." Jehovah-Raphah means "The Lord Who Heals." He is the I AM, which means the Self-Existent One or the Ever Present One. He has names that seem opposite in nature, but this is only because everything is summed up in Him. He is the God of Peace but also the Lord of Hosts revealing His militant nature. He is the Beginning and the End.

The importance of names extends even to cities. Remember my study of the seven churches began with the idea that the meaning of the city's name in which each church was located correlated to the message Christ gave them. Today, cities have reputations. Las Vegas is called "Sin City." Salt Lake City is synonymous with the Mormon religion. I believe the lack of a meaning of a city's name is also significant. Remember that Thyatira was of unknown meaning and that was significant in respect to the message given them. The same is true for Sardis. Its meaning is unknown. Even so, it had a name or reputation for being alive. In other words, this was a "happening" church. It probably had many programs and outreaches, good preaching, a large congregation, financial stability, gifts of the Spirit, and anything else that makes a church look alive in its community. Yet, Jesus said it was dead. Dead in the Greek is a corpse. A corpse is a shell that used to hold life. I've heard it said at funerals, "He looks like he is only sleeping." For a while, a corpse may look alive, but soon its stench and decay will let us know it is dead. The church at Sardis was an empty shell that hadn't yet started stinking except in God's nostrils.

What is amazing about this church is that it even had a good reputation with the citizens of Sardis. Remember, this was a time of intense persecution in the early church. John was in exile at Patmos. Many of his brothers in Christ had been martyred. During Nero's reign, Christians were used as torches at the games. The Romans viewed Christianity as a cult that molested children and practiced cannibalism. If a Christian, ministry, or church is not suffering some type of persecution, that could be a sign of living an ungodly life. Notice I said "could be." Persecution can come in cycles and from different sources. Some may experience persecution in the form of mocking from unsaved family members. Others may be treated unfairly at work for their Christian beliefs. Still others might experience persecution in the form of betrayal or slander from fellow believers. In fact, Paul told Timothy that "all who desire to live godly in Christ Jesus will suffer persecution" (2 Tim. 3:12). I believe the reason this church was not persecuted was because their lives were similar to the unsaved even though they continued in "church activity."

> And have no **fellowship** with the unfruitful **works** of darkness, but rather expose them. For it is shameful even to speak of those things which are done by them in secret. But all things are manifest by the light, for whatever makes manifest is light. Therefore He says: "Awake, you who **sleep, arise from the dead**, and Christ will give you light" (Eph. 5:11-14).

"Fellowship" means to share in company with, co-participate in.[2] Paul was telling the Ephesians not to co-participate with the "unfruitful works of darkness." Instead, they were to expose them. Remember, Jesus told this church, "I know your **works**." Participating in the works of darkness lulls a Christian to sleep like lullabies sung to babies. In the Bible, "sleep" is a word used to describe death (John 11:11,14, 2 Thess. 4:13-14, & 1 Cor. 15:20). We sleep at night; we work in the day. Crime is often committed at night. Adultery is committed under the cover of darkness (deception). We can't see as well in the dark. A corpse is buried and lies in the dark. When the Son of Man dawns as the sun, all those who are asleep (dead) in Christ will awaken to a new day.

The church at Sardis had been lulled to sleep by living like the world. They no longer influenced society but melted into society. I believe this condition describes the current condition of the western church. We have been like Hosea's prostitute wife Gomer who repeatedly went back to her lovers. We have continually committed adultery with our lovers—the gods of comfort, entertainment, money, sexual pleasure, and more. There has been no visible distinction between the unsaved and the saved. Because of this, the unsaved are confused and unimpressed by Christianity. Even so, God loved Gomer, and He loves us. In fact, God told Hosea to marry Gomer because his life was to be a testimony of God's love for His wayward people. Each time Gomer was unfaithful, Hosea was faithful to take her back when she returned. God promised to allure His people back to Himself and that in that day; they would call Him, "Husband." Even so, the people of God would experience trouble for their sins in the Valley of Achor (Achor means trouble) but the end would be singing as in the days of her youth when she first came out of Egypt. Hosea and Jesus both mean "Salvation." Like the ancient people of Israel, we, too, will go through the Valley of

Achor, but our end will be with singing as when we were first saved. Collectively, we are the Lord's bride, and He will perfect us and in the end, we will be without spot or wrinkle (Eph. 5:27).

The fact that Sardis looked good on the outside but was almost dead on the inside shows an important principle: you can't judge by external appearances. The Bible is full of examples of God's people judging others by external means instead of by their fruit. Saul was "a choice and handsome son (1 Sam. 9:2)." As a matter of fact, the Bible says that there was not any one more handsome than he (1 Sam. 8:2). The people loved Saul. Yet, he was rebellious (1 Sam. 15:10-23), demon possessed (1 Sam. 16:14), persecuted his son-in-law out of jealousy (1 Sam. 19), and killed 70 priests and their families (1 Sam. 22:6-21).

When Samuel went to Bethlehem to anoint the next king of Israel, he immediately thought David's brother Eliab was the next king, but God told him not to look at his appearance or his physical stature, because the Lord sees the heart of a man (1 Sam. 16:6,7). Jesus stated in John 5:30 that His judgment is righteous because He seeks the will of His Father over His own. In John 7:24 He commanded, "Do not judge according to appearance, but judge with righteous judgment." How do we judge (or discern) with righteous judgment? We seek the Father's will over our own like Jesus did. This is a lifestyle not an occasional decision.

For example, let's say that someone has offended you. Later you hear some gossip against that same person. Your flesh is tempted to judge them based on the gossip you heard because of your past experience with them and the resulting offense. But the Bible instructs us to not listen to gossip or to pick up an offense. The Bible also says that love believes the best (1 Cor. 13:7) and that love covers (Prov. 10:12). If you follow the Father's will written out in His Word, you will judge the situation righteously. Discernment simply means perception or judgment. Godly discernment is based in love (Phil. 1:9). If you discern something about someone, especially something negative, you must ask yourself whether you truly love that person. If you don't, you shouldn't trust your discernment. Often what people call discernment is nothing more than suspicion. Even so, there is a gift of discerning of spirits, which is the gift of determining what spirit is the true source of circumstances or motives of people. But the gift of discernment doesn't just discern the evil but the good. If you aren't discerning the Holy Spirit at work in other Christians, only demonic activity, you are out of balance. This can be especially difficult if the package is offensive. Jesus might work through a teenager with multiple piercing and tattoos. Are you humble enough to discern the Spirit when He speaks through this person?

The fact is a church can have great praise and worship, operate in the gifts of the Spirit, and have a large congregation but be spiritually deceased! It is also a fact that a person who names himself a Christian can go to church, serve in leadership, and tithe but have major sin in his life. In fact, this is a sign of the times. Paul warned us of perilous times in the last days in which Christians would have a form or appearance of godliness but be lovers of pleasure rather than God (2 Tim. 3:1-5). However, God promises in Malachi 3:16-18 that there will come a time when we will be able to discern between the righteous and the wicked. I call this "The Great Separation," and I believe it has started. In the last several years, I have seen many Christians' hidden sins exposed—everything ranging from drug abuse to murder. God promises that everything that is hidden will be exposed (Mt. 10:26). Because hidden sin is so rampant in the Body of Christ, it is important that we examine people's fruit not their gifts.

> A good tree cannot bear bad fruit, nor can a bad tree bear good fruit. Every tree that does not bear good fruit is cut down and thrown into the fire. Therefore by their fruits you will know them. Not everyone who says to Me, "Lord, Lord," shall enter the kingdom of heaven, but he who does the will of My Father in heaven. Many will say to Me in that day, "Lord, Lord, have we not prophesied in Your name, cast out demons in Your name, and done many wonders in Your name?" And then I will declare to them, "I never knew you; depart from Me, you who practice lawlessness" (Matt. 7:218-23)!

Church programs, prosperity, a large congregation, and even

miracles are not fruit. Galatians 5:22,23 says that "the fruit of the Spirit is love, joy, peace, longsuffering, kindness, goodness, faithfulness, gentleness, self-control." Practically, examining fruit takes time and often pressure. How does the individual act when his fruit is squeezed? Recently, a friend of mine has begun dating a man. She is a widow, and he has never been married. From talking with her, it seems this man is just right for her. He appears to be godly, patient, kind, peaceful, gentle, and faithful. Yet, I don't take only her word for it. I want to know what his friends and co-workers say about him. What is his work ethic? How has he acted during trials? Does he have fruit? I know of a pastor who calls the pastors, neighbors, and friends of anyone who wants to minister in his church to see what fruit he has. This might require more effort and time, but it is worth it.

Be Watchful

> Be watchful, and strengthen the things which remain, that are ready to die, for I have not found your works perfect before God. Remember therefore how you have received and heard; hold fast and repent. Therefore if you will not watch, I will come upon you as a thief and you will not know what hour I will come upon you (Rev. 3:2, 3).

"Watchful" means to keep awake.[3] Prior to Jesus' arrest, He asked the disciples to **watch** with Him for one hour, but they kept falling asleep (Mt. 26:40-45). This is the same word. Remember that living in darkness lulls one to sleep. Jesus told the disciples that watching and praying helps keep you from temptation (Mt. 26:41).

Being watchful simply means living in the Light (Eph. 5:13-15). Jesus' instruction to the church at Sardis was to wake up, strengthen what is still alive, and go back to what you know. If they refused, He warned them that He would come upon them as a thief. You never know when a thief will attack resulting in loss to you (Mt. 24:43, 44).

> But you, brethren, are not in darkness, so that this Day should overtake you as a thief. You are all sons of light

and sons of the day. We are not of the night nor of darkness. Therefore let us not **sleep,** as others do, but let us **watch** and be sober. For those who **sleep, sleep** at night, and those who get drunk are drunk at night (1 Thess. 5:4-7).

The warning to Sardis is similar to the language used to describe His second coming (Mt. 24:42, 43; 25:13; Mk. 13:35-37; 1 Thess. 5:2-6), and for this reason, I believe that the message to Sardis is a warning for all of the end-time church and reveals some of what is to come during this time. Let's read these two verses again plus the others that use similar language:

> Be watchful, and strengthen the things which remain, that are ready to die, for I have not found your works perfect before God. Remember therefore how you have received and heard; hold fast and repent. Therefore if you will not watch, I will come upon you as a thief and you will not know what hour I will come upon you (Rev. 3:2,3).
>
> **Watch** therefore, for **you do not know what hour your Lord is coming**. But know this, that if the master of the house had known what **hour the thief** would come, he would have **watched** and not allowed his house to be broken into. Therefore you also be ready, for the Son of Man is coming at an hour you do not expect (Matt. 24:42-44).
>
> **Watch** therefore, for you know neither the day nor the hour in which the Son of Man is coming… **Watch** therefore, for you know neither the day nor the hour in which the Son of Man is coming (Matt. 25:13).
>
> **Watch** therefore, for you do not know when the master of the house is coming—in the evening, at midnight, at the crowing of the rooster, or in the morning—lest, coming suddenly, he find you sleeping. And what I say to you, I say to all: Watch (Mk. 13:35-37)!

> For you yourselves know perfectly that the day of the Lord so comes as a **thief in the night**…But you, brethren, are not in darkness, so that this Day should overtake you as a thief…Therefore let us not **sleep**, as others do, but let us **watch** and be sober (1 Thess. 5:2, 4, 6).

As this age closes, a deep darkness is going to cover the earth. Darkness represents deception and lawlessness, so in other words, it's going to get worse before it gets better. However, the Lord's glory will arise on His people (Isa. 60:1-3). What is interesting about light is that darkness cannot overcome it (Jn. 1:5). No matter how dark a room, the darkness flees when the light is turned on. Also, the darker it is, the brighter the light and easier to see. Isaiah tells us that the Gentiles, a term for the unsaved, will come to our light and kings to the brightness of our rising. It will finally be clear who has the real Light—not the New Age believers, the Buddhists, the Muslims but the Christians.

> But the path of the just is like the shining sun, that shines ever brighter unto the perfect day. The way of the wicked is like darkness; they do not know what makes them stumble (Prov. 4:18, 19).

All Christians should be shining brighter more than the previous year. At first, you might only shine a tad more, but as you mature in the Lord, the degree of your brightness dramatically increases due to learning obedience and knowing Him better. If you are not getting brighter each year, then you need to examine what is wrong. Often you can pinpoint the problem to what you allow in and out of your soul. For example, when you are first saved, it probably won't bother you to watch the same movies you watched before you were saved. However, over time, the Holy Spirit will convict you that your eyes are the windows into your soul, so what you let in by watching these ungodly movies is not light. You slowly begin to be more selective and cut out horror movies. After a little time has gone by, you then are convicted of movies that have sexual content in them. You cut them out. Then you are bothered by movies with excessive cussing. There they go. Then any cussing bothers you. You see, it is a progress, but there should be some improvement. As you begin to close the doors to any darkness in your life, you get brighter.

Our goal as time progresses is to remain in the light. Scientists have studied individuals who work nightshifts and have found that their bodies are naturally sleepy at night no matter how many hours they sleep in the day and how brightly lit the room. I can attest to this. The fact is that when it is dark outside, your body eventually wants to sleep. God made us that way. As believers, we would be wise to understand that as the darkness covers the earth, we will get sleepy. The apostles experienced this when Jesus asked them to watch with Him before His crucifixion (Matt. 26:40, 43, 45). In their case, it wasn't only the fact that it was nighttime that made them sleepy, but also the overwhelming sense of sorrow. We have to be careful to not be overwhelmed by the sin we will see flaunted before our eyes (Lk. 21:34). It will seem that darkness is overcoming light, but the darker it gets, the closer to dawn we are. You see, in the natural, nighttime is the darkest and coldest right before the dawn. God is warning us through natural events that right before He dawns as the Morning Star (sun) on humanity again (2 Pet. 1:19; Rev. 22:16), it is going to be the darkest and the coldest that it has ever been in the history of humanity.

> But to you who fear My name the **Sun of Righteousness shall arise** with healing in His wings; and you shall go out and grow fat like stall-fed calves (Mal. 4:2).

With all of this established, we can better understand what Jesus was saying to the church at Sardis, "Wake up. Watch. Get up and strengthen that which remains but is almost asleep (dead). You have been fellowshipping with the fruits of darkness so your works are not perfect before Me." And then He warns them:

> Remember therefore how you have received and heard; hold fast and repent. Therefore **if you will not watch, I will come upon you as a thief, and you will not know what hour I will come upon you** (Rev. 2:3).

Prophecy in the Bible usually has an immediate fulfillment and a future fulfillment. The immediate fulfillment occurs during the lifetime of the one receiving the prophecy, and the future fulfillment is for later. This is seen repeatedly in Old Testament prophecies in which the day of the Lord and His first and second coming was combined with prophecies about specific countries of that day. I believe the same is the case for the warning given to Sardis in that they needed to repent so that they escaped an unexpected historical judgment. Even so, the language He uses is very much "end-time" in nature considering the words He used here are similar to those He used in speaking about His second coming (Matt. 24:42-44; 25:13; Mk. 13:33, 35-37; Lk. 21:34-36).

The parable of the wise and foolish virgins intrigues and concerns me. It concerns me because all ten of the virgins fall asleep while the bridegroom was delayed. And all of them heard the cry that the bridegroom is coming. Also, they all trimmed their wicks. The *only* difference between the wise and foolish is the wise carried extra oil. To better understand what this parable means to the end-time church, we must examine the history of the culture of Jesus' day.

When a young man wanted to marry a young girl, he approached the father and asked for permission. If the father granted permission, the man left and went to build a home suitable for his bride if he didn't already have one. Remember Jesus told the disciples that He was going to prepare a place for us (John 14:2). When the home was built, he announced that he was ready for his bride. His best friend then ran through the village proclaiming that the bridegroom was ready for his bride. The bridegroom joined by friends and relatives journeyed to the house of his bride and joyfully led her in a procession to his house. According to Jewish custom, about ten lamps carried on staves were used as the bride was led to her home. And at formal banquets, once all the guests arrived and proved they were invited, the "master of the house" shut the door and no matter how insistent no one entered after the door was shut. Ancient Middle Eastern custom shows us that the initial nuptial ceremonies began at midnight, which supports the parable's text, which says that the cry that the bridegroom was coming occurred at midnight.

Obviously, the bridegroom is none other than the Lord Jesus. He has been preparing our home for 2,000 years, but during this time, the church has slowly fallen asleep. That doesn't seem to bother Jesus as He relates the parable. When the last stone is in place (1 Pet. 2:5), He will notify the Father that He is done. The Holy Spirit will then cry out that the bridegroom is coming waking the church from her slumber. *All Christians throughout the earth will get up and trim their lamps.* The word trimmed is *kosmeo*, and it means, "to beautify, arrange, decorate, furnish, adorn, or **put in order**." From the time of the cry that the bridegroom is coming and His actual appearance, there is time to quickly put on the finishing touches of our wedding garments. But something happens to five of the virgins—their lamps are running out of oil, which means their light will go out. Frantic, they ask the wise for some of their extra oil, but the wise prudently decline lest they run out also. This tells me that from the initial cry of the Holy Spirit that the Bridegroom is coming, there will be the waiting for Him to actually get here just like the bridegroom journeyed from his home to fetch his bride.

The foolish virgins hurriedly leave to go out and buy some oil, but while they were gone, the bridegroom comes. It says, "…those who were ready went in with him to the wedding and the door was shut. Afterward the other virgins came also, saying, 'Lord, Lord, open to us!' But he answered and said, 'Assuredly, I say to you, I do not know you'" (Mt. 25:10b-12). It is my opinion that all Christians will hear the cry of His coming and attempt to put in order their lives, but last minute changes do not produce Christ-likeness. The outward appearance of the foolish virgins may look like the wise virgins', but it is not the same. The wise virgins spent years getting ready by studying His Word and getting to know Him through prayer. These matured and disposed of the unfruitful works of darkness in their life resulting in a surplus of oil for the final waiting period before He arrived. Oil represents the presence of the Holy Spirit and His anointing.

> See then that you walk circumspectly (carefully), not as **fools** but as **wise**, redeeming the time, because the days are evil. Therefore do not be unwise, but **understand what the will of the Lord is**, and do not be drunk with wine in which is dissipation; but be **filled** with the Spirit (Eph. 5:15-18).

Filled is not a one-time event of being baptized in the Holy

Spirit. The tense of *be filled* literally means to "continually be filled." How? Verse 19 tells us one of the best ways to be ever filled: worship through song using psalms, hymns, and other spiritual songs. This is to be done corporately and personally. I believe another way is in-depth study in which the Son of God is revealed to you in new and intimate ways by the Holy Spirit (Jn. 14:26).

The Right Garments

> You have a few names even in Sardis who have not defiled their garments; and they shall walk with Me in white, for they are worthy (Rev. 3:4).

Garments speak of righteousness or of sin. "Defiled" means soiled in the Greek.[4] Jude 23 talks about "hating the garment defiled by the flesh." Revelation 19:8 says, "And to her (the bride) it was granted to be arrayed in fine linen, clean and bright, for the fine linen is the righteous acts of the saints." And in Zechariah 3:3, 4, God removes Joshua's filthy garments that represented his iniquity, and He clothed him in rich robes. But to better understand the significance of garments, we again need to look at another parable about a wedding in Matthew 22:1-14, the parable of the wedding feast.

In this parable, a king arranged a marriage for his son. He sent out his servants to call those who were initially invited to the wedding feast but all gave excuses. The Bible says they that "made light of it," which means neglected in the Greek. Some of the invited even killed the king's servants. These the king destroyed. Then he sent out other servants to invite those who were not worthy, which speaks of the Gentiles or non-Jews, and the wedding hall was filled. But then something interesting happens.

> But when the king came in to see the guests, he saw a man there who did not have on a wedding garment. So he said to him, "Friend, how did you come in here without a wedding garment?" And he was speechless (Mt. 22:11-12).

The king had this man bound and cast into outer darkness. Jesus then explains that many are called but few chosen. This ending may seem odd, but again you have to understand the culture of His time. First, the king is the father, and the son is Jesus. The initial guests were the Israelites, but they rejected His Son. Therefore, the father invited all Gentiles into His kingdom through salvation. But even then, there will be some who will try to enter the wedding feast in the wrong garments. In ancient times, king and princes gave garments as presents to their favorite people. To refuse this gift was an expression of highest contempt. It was expected that the favored were to wear their new garments in the presence of the king. The garments were chiefly long white robes.[5] The man in the parable wore his common, ordinary dress refusing the wonderful robe from the king, which showed utter contempt.

Those who are chosen are those who have allowed the Holy Spirit to transform them into the image of the Son (Rom. 8:29). Their garments are no longer soiled by sin but are instead white by their righteous acts of obedience from love. In Sardis, there was a remnant that had not defiled their garments with iniquity. God always has a remnant, which He has made clear in both of these wedding parables.

THE PROMISE

> He who overcomes shall be clothed in white garments,
> and I will not blot out his name from the Book of Life;
> but I will confess his name before My Father and before
> His angels (Rev. 3:5).

Again, Jesus stresses that the Christians who overcome will be clothed in white garments, which denotes favor and a race finished well (2 Tim. 4:7; Heb. 12:1). But notice the next promise, "...and I will not blot out his name from the Book of Life; but I will confess his name before My Father and before His angels." This promise or the complications of not overcoming should put the fear of God in you.

Jesus told His disciples not to rejoice that demons are subject to them but instead that their names are written in heaven (Matt. 10:20). This book determines our future. Revelation 20:15 describes God looking in His book, the *Book of Life*, to determine whether a person is a part of His family. If your name is not in that book, your eternal future is doomed to the lake of fire. But in the promise given to the church at Sardis, He was pointing out that a believer's name can be blotted out. The word blot means literally to wipe out or wipe off. It can be likened to using a pencil eraser to erase a mistake. In other words, it is possible to lose one's salvation. Before you get scared that you might have already lost your salvation, let's examine how this might happen.

> Not everyone who says to Me, "Lord, Lord," shall enter the kingdom of heaven, but he who does the will of My Father in heaven. Many will say to Me in that day, "Lord, Lord, have we not prophesied in Your name, cast out demons in Your name, and done many wonders in Your name?" And then I will declare to them, "I never knew you; depart from Me, you who practice lawlessness" (Mt. 7:21-23)!

The key to understanding how something like this could happen is the word "practice" in verse 23. "Practice makes perfect," is a true saying. The more you do something, the better you are at it. If you practice obedience, you will mature in righteousness. If you practice disobedience, which is what lawlessness means in the Greek, you will mature in sin. Lawlessness is simply having fellowship with the unfruitful works of darkness. It is outright rebellion versus immaturity. The immature are slowly being changed, but the rebellious refuse to change. Repeated acts of rebellion or stiff-arming God put the believer in a dangerous position. And notice that these same Christians worked miracles, but miracles or operating in gifts won't save you. Jesus told us to examine each other's fruit because that's what He does. I think this is also a wonderful picture of the foolish virgins who lived their lives how they saw fit and the door was closed to them.

It is also important to notice that He will confess our name before the Father and His angels. Confess literally means to agree fully. This scripture reminds me of formal parties I've seen on television. Whenever a guest arrived, the butler announced the guest's name to the other party goers. Well, we're invited to a party—the wedding feast. It would go well with us if Jesus can vouch for us to the Father so we're not kicked out!

> Also I say to you, whoever confesses Me before men,
> him the Son of Man also will confess before the angels
> of God (Lk. 12:8).

Knowing that confess means to agree fully, we must agree fully with Christ on this earth! Our thoughts, words, actions, and works must be in agreement with Him and His Word. It is not enough to just say you are a Christian; you must live like a Christian. As Amos 3:3 puts it, "Can two walk together, unless they are agreed?"

> This is a faithful saying: For if we died with Him, we
> shall also live with Him. If we endure, we shall also
> reign with Him. If we deny Him, He also will deny us. If
> we are faithless, He remains faithful; He cannot deny
> Himself (2 Tim. 2:11-13).

God is faithful. If we deny Him, He cannot deny Himself by accepting those into His kingdom who have rejected Him. He is faithful even when it will break His heart. What most don't understand is that denying Him isn't so much saying, "I deny Jesus Christ." Titus tells us that one way to deny Him is by our works—works that are abominable, disobedient, and disqualifying (1:16). Again, this is describing those who "practice lawlessness."

APPLICATION

I feel the message to the church at Sardis is especially vital to churches in America and Western Europe today. All over the world, there are dead churches. However, we live in a society of prosperity and gross wickedness much like those in Sardis. Because of this, we must be careful not to be lulled to sleep by the darkness of our cultures. We must be watchful. We must stay in the Word and obey it. We must cleave to Christ living in His light. We must get to know Him in prayer, which is a dialogue, not a monologue. We must live carefully.

Leaders of ministries and especially churches must be cautious of using programs, hype, and entertainment to lure the people. Numbers do not mean you are alive. Fruit does. A dead fruit tree will not bear fruit. Are you alive? Do you have fruit in your life? Is your church or ministry bearing fruit in the lives of others? If not, repent, strengthen that which is alive, hold fast to what you originally learned that led you to the Lord and helped you mature, and watch and pray.

7 PHILADELPHIA

And to the angel of the church in Philadelphia write...
(Revelation 3:7)

The city of Philadelphia was a city of ancient Lydia in Asia Minor. According to the *International Standard Bible Encyclopedia*, Philadelphia was known for its excellent wine produced from exceedingly fertile land that the famed Roman poet, Virgil, wrote about.[1] Philadelphia is not as old as its counterparts, but it quickly grew as an important and wealthy trade center. As other coastal cities declined, Philadelphia grew in power until the late Byzantine times despite frequent earthquakes.

"Philadelphia" means love of brethren.[2] It was named in honor of Attalus II because of his loyalty to his brother. The church at Philadelphia is one of only two churches, the other being Smyrna, that did not receive a rebuke from Jesus Christ. I believe it is because the church here lived up to its name—love of brethren.

Today, Philadelphia is a city in modern Turkey named Ala-Shehir—"the city of God." It is still a Christian town, and a Greek bishop makes his home there. Its chief modern industry is licorice. The best way to reach Philadelphia is by rail from Smyrna, which I believe is significant. Jesus showed His love (Philadelphia) for His brethren (Israel) and His future brethren (Gentiles) by enduring persecution (Smyrna) including death on the cross. Jesus said in John 15:13, "Greater love has no one than this, than to lay down one's life for his friends." But in order to have this brotherly love, one must first love God (1 John 2:5, 3:10, 11, 16-19 and John 14:21).

Right after Jesus made His statement in John 15:13, He says in verse 14, "You are My friends if you do whatever I command you." According to John 14:21 those who love God do what He says. He also told us that the greatest commandment is to love God with your whole being, and the second commandment is to love your neighbor as yourself. On these two commandments hang all the Law and the Prophets (Matt. 22:36-40). If you love, you will fulfill His commandments and your calling. But what is interesting is in John 14 after He made the statements about loving one another (vv. 13-17), He then describes in detail the world's hatred for us and our coming persecution. Genuine God-love and persecution are usually companions. One reason for this is that Satan hates love because God is love, and he hates anything to do with God and His characteristics. Also, love isn't an emotional feeling but a lifestyle of choosing God's ways above our own comfort, which sometimes means confronting wrongs that are hurting others. Jesus continually did this while He was in the flesh. As His body, we now continue His work.

Growing in brotherly love (phileo) and full-grown God-love (agape) takes time. When an individual is born again and Spirit-filled, the Holy Spirit pours into his heart the love (agape) of God (Rom. 5:5). How? We must understand that when we are born again, God enters our spirit as the Divine Seed in Spirit form (1 Jn. 3:9). All that He is, including love, now resides in our spirits, but it is in seed form. As we are in the Word, pray, and have fellowship with others, the seed matures, and we begin to look more like Him. This is why the different characteristics of God are listed as fruit of the *Spirit* in Galatians 5:22 and 23 because fruit must develop. Second Peter 1:5-8 describes this process of maturing.

> But also for this very reason, giving all diligence, add to your faith virtue, to virtue knowledge, to knowledge self-control, to self-control perseverance, to perseverance godliness, to godliness **brotherly**

> **kindness**, and to brotherly kindness **love**. For if these things are yours and abound, **you will be neither barren nor unfruitful** in the knowledge of our Lord Jesus Christ.

Notice that this process takes diligence, which is eagerness and earnestness. You begin with faith that Christ is the Son of God. As He matures you, you then begin to walk in virtue, which is excellence—excellence in your job, study, dress, conversation, and every other area of your life. Then your knowledge of God increases. With this knowledge comes self-control. Things you might have done in the past, you don't do anymore because of your knowledge of the Word and obedience to it and God. Self-control then paves the way for perseverance, which is patience. Patience is not simply waiting for something, but it is waiting with a good attitude whether you're in a checkout line at the store or believing for something through prayer. Patience is only developed by trials and tribulations, which can include a checkout line! After patience begins to develop, godliness forms. Another word for godliness is holiness. In order to be holy, we must know Him as holy. This produces fear of the Lord, and a proper fear of the Lord causes us not to sin (Ex. 20:20). After all of these things are developed, then comes brotherly love and finally agape love. One way to tell the difference between the two is that brotherly love is often conditional based on if the person is pleasing you. Agape love is unconditional, by choice, and always seeks the best for the other person. This is the epitome of Christ.

Many in their early Christian walk confuse the love they feel for God for agape love. Peter did this also. He knew that he loved Jesus as a brother and was, therefore, willing to die for Him. I truly believed that Peter would have laid down his life for Jesus because he fearlessly cut off the ear of the high priest's servant when they came to arrest Him (Jn. 18:10). But when Jesus healed the servant's ear and allowed them to take Him, Peter was confronted with a love higher than his, which he didn't understand. All he thought he knew about Jesus was shaken, and he fell (Lk. 22:31, 32; Jn. 18:15-18, 25-27).

After Jesus' resurrection, He sought to restore Peter. He asked him what appears to be the same question three times, but He used *phileo* and *agape* for love. In John 21:15, Jesus asked Peter if He loved Him. He used the word *agape*. Peter responded by saying that he loved Him, but he used *phileo*, so in essence, he was saying, "I have affection for you." Jesus asked him again using *agape*, and Peter responded the same. Finally, Jesus asked him a third time and this time, He used *phileo* for love. He met Peter where he was and still gave him the commission to feed His lambs and sheep and tend to them (vv.15-17). He also wanted to make sure Peter was honest about his love for Him, and Peter was, indeed, humbled and knew where he was spiritually. We all begin with affection for the Lord, and often our love is selfishly motivated. We must understand that *agape* love is seen by our obedience to Him even when we are uncomfortable or do not understand (Jn. 14:21). As we grow in this, we begin to love others with God's love.

Even with all this said, do not feel condemned that you are not walking in *agape* love yet. Ask yourself, "Do I have faith that Jesus is the Son of God?" If so, you are on your way because it begins with faith. Even if you have only this one thing, according to Second Peter 1:5-8, you will mature into the other if you remain diligent.

GREETING

> These things says He who is holy, He who is true. 'He who has the key of David, He who opens and no one shuts, and shuts and no one opens'" (Revelation 3:7).

In order to understand this verse, we must go to where John is quoting from, which is Isaiah 22:22. The context behind this verse is important also. At the time, King Hezekiah's "second-in-command" was a man named Shebna. He is called his steward (Isa. 22:15), which is basically someone in charge of a household including the financial aspects. *Webster's New World Dictionary and Thesaurus* says a steward is "a person morally responsible for the careful use of money, time, talents, or other resources, esp. with respect to principles or needs of a community or group." Another definition is "a person put in charge of the affairs of a large household or estate, whose duties include supervision of the kitchen and the servants, management of household accounts, etc." In the King James Version, "steward" is translated treasurer. Shebna held the powerful position of being the steward over the king's house including the finances necessary in running the household. The king granted Shebna power and position. These two things caused Shebna to think too much of himself and fall into the sin of pride.

> Go, proceed to this steward, to Shebna, who is over the house, and say: "What have you here, and whom have you here, that you have hewn a sepulcher here, as he who hews himself in a rock. Indeed, the Lord will throw you away violently, O mighty man, and will surely seize you. He will surely turn violently and toss you like a ball into a large country; there you shall die, and there your glorious chariots shall be the shame of your master's house. So I will drive you out of your office, and from your position he will pull you down" (Isa. 22:15-19).

Basically, Isaiah asked Shebna whom he thought he was that he was having his sepulcher carved out of the rock like he was royalty or something. You see, it was the custom of kings to have impressive sepulchers carved out of rock for themselves and their families. Shebna was not of royalty so his act was a form of pride not honor. He wanted this immortality so that when anyone saw his sepulcher, they would comment on how he must have been a great man. Instead of being satisfied with the authority and rule granted him, he wanted to be as royalty. For his pride, he was promised a fall and exile.

> "Then it shall be in that day, that I will call My **servant** Eliakim the **son** of Hilkiah; I will clothe him with your robe and strengthen him with your belt; I will commit your responsibility into his hand. He shall be a father to the inhabitants of Jerusalem and to the house of Judah. The key of the house of David I will lay upon his shoulder; so he shall open, and no one shall shut; and he shall shut, and no one shall open. I will fasten him as a peg in a secure place, and he will become a glorious throne to his father's house" (Isa. 22:20-23).

Interestingly, "Shebna" means to grow in the Hebrew,[3] but instead of growing in humility from a steward to a servant, he grew prideful. "Eliakim" means God is raising.[4] Anytime we get prideful, God will raise someone else to replace us. This is an important lesson for us as Christians. When we are first born again, we begin as stewards. This means that we pretty much continue to do whatever we want with our time and money. But as we grow in our relationship with the Lord, a heart change takes place where we begin to understand that everything we "own" is actually God's, which is the servant stage. Even so, God wants us to go even deeper in our relationship and transform us into bondservants. This means that even though we have freedom to do whatever we want with what we have, we instead choose to submit it all to Him and His will. This submission includes all things. You see, a servant is free to do whatever he desires on his free time, but a bondservant chooses to seek the master's will about what to do on his free time. Does this mean we can't have fun? No, but it means that we are careful to listen to the still, small voice of the Holy Spirit.

> I am the good shepherd. The good shepherd gives His life for the sheep. **But a hireling, he who is not the shepherd, one who does not own the sheep,** sees the wolf coming and leaves the sheep and flees; and the wolf catches the sheep and scatters them. **The hireling flees because he is a hireling and does not care about the sheep.** I am the good shepherd; and I know My sheep, and am known by My own (John 10:11-14).

Like Shebna, the religious leaders of Jesus' time thought of themselves more highly than they should have. They were placed in charge of God's people, but they ruled with the hearts of hirelings. They didn't care about the sheep, and they were full of pride (John 9:34-10:1-18). Therefore, God raised up Another to be over His household—His Son. Remember, Eliakim means "God of raising." Not only was Jesus placed in the exalted position as Shepherd over God's household, but He was also raised from the dead. God, indeed, raised Christ spiritually and physically.

What happened to Shebna? Not many details are given, but we

can be assured that the prophecy of Shebna's downfall was literally fulfilled. The only clue we have of this is in Isaiah 36:3, which states that Eliakim is over the household, and a man named Shebna is listed as a scribe. If this is the same Shebna described in Isaiah 22, it shows that he was demoted to the position of scribe. His exile might have come later.

Prophetically, the religious leaders of Jesus' time encountered the same fate as Shebna. Their refusal to recognize Jesus as their Messiah affected the entire nation of Israel. As a nation, Israel was thrown away violently when in 70 A.D., the Roman army completely destroyed Jerusalem and sent all Jews into exile. Remember that in Isaiah 22:18, God said He would throw Shebna like a ball into a large country. "Country" can also mean earth.[5] After the Romans destroyed Israel, the Israelites were scattered throughout the earth for almost 2,000 years. Even so, God desires to restore Israel by re-grafting them back into a covenantal relationship. For this reason, He has been guiding Jews all over the world to return to Palestine. This process began after Israel was reformed into a nation after World War II, something that had never before been done in history.

Key of David

In ancient times, keys were carried on the shoulder. They were much larger than our keys today, usually six inches to two feet long. They were made of wood often with a handle of brass or silver ornamented with filigree work. To place keys on a person's shoulder was giving that person responsibility over what doors those keys locked and opened. It signified the person's position. Also, in ancient times, the steward of a wealthy family or a royal family was given a golden key in recognition of his office.

Revelation 3:7 says that Jesus has the key of David. Why David? David established a kingdom that reflected the heart of God. He united the two kingdoms of Judah and Israel. He established a system of worship in which prayer and music was heard and played 24 hours a day unto God. The ark was housed in a tent where anyone who desired to worship God could enter and do so. This was unprecedented for the ark had always been hidden from Israel as a whole. His whole life was to seek the Lord. David lived in the future age of grace during the age of the

Law. David's administration as shepherd over Israel established the throne on which Jesus would sit (2 Sam. 7:12-16; Lk. 1:32, 33). Thrones represent authority and so do keys. That is why Jesus has the key of David.

> For unto us a Child is born, unto us a **Son** is given; **and the government will be upon His shoulder**, and His name will be called Wonderful, Counselor, Mighty God, **Everlasting Father,** Prince of Peace. Of the increase of His government and peace there will be no end, upon the throne of David and over His kingdom, to order it and establish it with judgment and justice from that time forward, even forever. The zeal of the Lord of hosts will perform this (Isa. 9:6-7).

The phrase, "the government…upon His shoulder," is a direct reference to the keys that would sit upon the shoulder of the servant of the household. That authority He also extended to His kingdom people.

> And I will give you the keys of the kingdom of heaven, and whatever you bind on earth will be bound in heaven, and whatever you loose on earth will be loosed in heaven (Matt. 16:19).

Literally, this verse says that whatever you bind on earth must have already been bound in heaven, and whatever you loose on earth must have already been loosed in heaven. Whenever we go about kingdom business as His representatives, we are not to use the keys for our personal gain, and we shouldn't be prideful. Instead, we must work in partnership with the Lord to further His kingdom rule; therefore, we must get our directives from the throne and carry them out on this earth. In other words, the kingdom business we do must already be established in heaven or be the will of heaven. This is what Jesus meant when He said that He only did what He saw His Father do.

EXORTATION

> I know your works. See, I have set before you an open door, and no one can shut it; for you have a little

strength, have kept My word, and have not denied My name (Revelation 3:8).

The church at Philadelphia had works of light, which prompted the Lord to open a door for them that no man could shut. Some believe that He opened a door of opportunity to spread the gospel or a door of service (1 Cor. 16:9; 2 Cor. 2:12). These things may apply, but I believe this door was prophetic revelation.

> After these things I looked, and behold, **a door standing open in heaven**. And the first voice which I heard was like a trumpet speaking with me, saying, **"Come up here, and I will show you things which must take place after this"** (Rev. 4:1).

As stated, Philadelphia means "brotherly love." The author of the book of Revelation is the Apostle John. The reason these two things are important is that John has often been called the Apostle of Love, and it was he who was invited to experience prophetic revelation of the end of this age. Remember, he was the one who laid his head on Jesus' chest (Jn. 13:23). He is the only disciple who didn't abandon Jesus when He was arrested (Jn. 18:15). And the epistle of First John is filled with the exhortations to love God and one another. Why is this important? It is important because a key to experiencing an "open heaven" is love for God and for others. Even so, it is also important to understand that we can't initiate an "open heaven" experience. This is a door only the Lord can open; however, we will never experience the closeness with Him required for an open door if we are not walking in love.

> He who has My commandments and keeps them, **it is he who loves Me**. And he who loves Me will be loved by My Father, and I will love him and **manifest Myself** to him. Judas (not Iscariot) said to Him, "Lord, how is it that You will manifest Yourself to us, and not to the world?" Jesus answered and said to him, "If anyone loves Me, **he will keep My word**; and My Father will love him, and We will come to him and **make Our home with him.** He who does not love Me does not

keep My words; and the word which you hear is not
Mine but the Father's who sent me" (Jn. 14:21-24).

Here the Lord reveals that loving Him is directly related to obeying Him. This is a test to see if we truly love Him—are we doing what He says? As this love deepens and grows, something will happen in our spirits and in the heavenlies in which a door of intimacy with Him is opened. Jesus said, "I will…manifest Myself to him [who loves Me]." He even told the disciples that He would make His home with those who love Him. You see, He may live in you now because you are born again, but the real question is, "Is He at home in you?" In other words, are you living a life of obedience in which He is at rest in your spirit. We must understand that we are not our own. God lives in us! This means that the things we say, think, and do affect not just us but Him. Think of love as being the hinges of the door of revelation. If you are in obedience, they will be well oiled allowing intimacy with God and prophetic revelation to flow freely.

The Lord then continues His encouragement by praising them for keeping His word, not denying His name, and maintaining some strength. But then He gives them an amazing promise that is a direct result of their love for Him and His for them. Read these words and hear the fierce protectiveness in His voice.

> Indeed, I will make those of the synagogue of Satan, who say they are Jews, and are not, but lie—**indeed I will make them come and worship before your feet, and to know that I have loved you** (Rev. 3:9).

What a wonderful promise! You see, the believers at Philadelphia probably endured much persecution from the Jews that lived there. Obviously, there was a synagogue, and Jesus' strong language by calling it a "synagogue of Satan" shows His displeasure with mere religion and religious men for those who have religion minus relationship with God always persecute Jesus' body on this earth just like they literally killed Him 2,000 years ago. We must understand that religion such as what persecuted Him and these believers is an evil spirit sent from Satan to destroy. But those who worshiped religion more than

God will one day worship the true God at the true believers' feet. For this reason, if you are being persecuted by anyone with a religious spirit, do a "hallelujah jig" for you are enduring the same persecution as the Lord Jesus Christ!

The Hour of Trial

> Because you have kept My command to persevere, I also will keep you from the hour of trial which shall come upon the whole world, to test those who dwell on the earth (Rev. 3:10).

What I'm about to share with you might make you uncomfortable. But let me state that all true good teachers will leave you with more questions than answers. The reason for this is that everyone receives teaching and prophecy in part (1 Cor. 13:9). The Lord designed His church this way so that we had to have each other and be in unity. Therefore, good teachers will raise questions and a desire in you to dig deeper in His word. Now, of course, this might result in you becoming very busy searching the scriptures, but what better past time is there? Remember, it is the glory of God to hide something but the glory of kings to search it out (Prov. 25:2).

With this said, I want to humbly suggest to you that much that is taught about the end times in the body is short-sighted at best and flat wrong at worst. Even so, there are some truths in the teachings out there, so it is our responsibility to "rightly divide the word of truth" (2 Tim. 2:15). Also understand as you read the following that I am not in any way claiming to know all there is to know about the end times. But what little I have learned in studying for almost 20 years, I will share with you here. I ask that you allow me to lay my foundation, and then you can pray and search the scriptures yourself to see if you agree or not. Much of my information came from *Zodhiates: The Complete Word Study Dictionary New Testament*.

First, let me state that Revelation 3:10 is often used to support the "pre-tribulation rapture" doctrine, which is a teaching that states that believers will be raptured by Jesus before the seven-year tribulation and the coming of the beast or antichrist. This doctrine also states that Jesus can return for His church at any minute. Once the church is removed, all hell will break lose on earth as the enemy wreaks havoc through the beast and his cohorts. They say this will also be a time when the wrath of God is poured upon unbelievers.

As stated, there are some things in the "pre-trib rapture" doctrine that is correct, but I believe the scriptures clearly show many reasons why this doctrine just doesn't fit perfectly with the end-time plan of God. You see, prophecy is like a puzzle. You can't force a piece to fit where it doesn't belong. Much of the confusion comes from a lack of digging into the original language of key words and phrases. For this reason, I dug as far as I could to understand exactly what Jesus was saying here in Revelation 3:10.

With this understanding, let's first ask ourselves why did Jesus even tell the Philadelphian believers they would be kept from the hour of trial coming upon the whole earth knowing that when that time came, they would all be dead? His reason goes back to what we first learned, which is that the things He spoke to the seven churches in Revelation can apply to individual churches throughout history and even different church periods in history. This means that the Lord was letting them know that at the time of their persecution, He would take care of them, but He was also letting us know thousands of years later that those who live as the believers at Philadelphia will also be kept from the hour of trial. Now, let's see exactly what He meant.

The first word I want to examine in Revelation 3:10 is the word "from." There are two Greek words for "from," which are *apo* and *ek*. In this verse, "from" is *ek*, but I want to first examine *apo* before we discuss *ek*. *Apo* is a Greek word that means that you never enter something or that you are kept out of something completely.[6] For example, let's say you get up one morning and are running late for work. Everything fights you. You can't find your keys, your car has a flat, and your cell phone doesn't work. You finally start for work and discover that at the exact time you should have been on the freeway, there was a horrific wreck that you might have been involved in. God kept you from (*apo*) that wreck completely.

Now, let's look at *ek*. *Ek* means out of, from, of, as spoken of such objects which were before in another.[7] A good illustration of *ek* is a glass within a glass. The smaller glass is removed and used for orange juice; the larger glass is used for vinegar. While both remain in use, one is for sweet orange juice, and the other is used for the bitter vinegar. If we use our wreck example, it is being in the wreck but coming out unscathed. Jesus was saying, "Because you have done what I've said and persevered in the midst of persecution, I will take you **out of** the hour of trial that is coming." In other words, we will be in the midst as the smaller glass was in the midst of the larger glass and then removed. We will then enjoy **sweet** salvation of the Lord, but those on the earth will be experiencing the **bitterness** of the wrath of God.

A Biblical example of *ek* is the Israelites in Egypt during the ten plagues. The Israelites were in the midst of the plagues but were not touched by them. God didn't rapture them right before the plagues. That would have been *apo*. Instead, He protected them and eventually led them **out of** (*ek*) Egypt, which resulted in the destruction of Pharaoh's army. This is a perfect picture of what will happen with the church when the hour of trial comes. The church will be taken **out of** the hour of trial not before. Only the Lord knows how long we will remain in the hour of trial.

Another important word to understand is "keep." "Keep" is *tereo* and means "to guard from loss or injury…by keeping the eye upon."[8] Again, this implies that we will be within the hour of trial, but God will keep such a close eye on us that He will guard us from the loss and injury the world will sustain. This guarding would not be necessary if we were already raptured and in heaven. The protection the Israelites had in Egypt applies here as well. While the Egyptians experienced definite injury and loss from God's wrath, the Israelites were safe. Hopefully, you see that by Jesus using the words He did for "keep" and "from," He was assuring us protection in the midst of difficult times.

Now we need to examine what the hour of trial is. First, the word "hour" simply means a short time or brief interval such as an hour or it can mean a day, a season, time, or instant.[9] Jesus used this word in Matthew 24:42-44 when He cautioned His disciples that they did not know the hour He was returning. He explained that if a homeowner knew when the thief would strike, he would have watched and been ready. He then warned them that He would return at an hour we would not expect. I believe this had immediate fulfillment and applies to our times.

Back then, historians have discovered that the early church expected the Lord to return during their lifetime and some concern arose over the fact that some of them had already died, and He still hadn't returned. Paul addressed this concern in his first letter to the believers at Thessalonica by explaining that those who had died would still be a part of the Lord's return. In fact, he stated that they would be resurrected first (1 Thess. 4:13-15). Because of the confusion on the timing of His return, part of Matthew 24:44 was fulfilled in that the early believers definitely didn't expect Him to *not* return during their lifetime.

Peter also addressed this problem of Him not returning when we expect Him in his second letter. He warned that scoffers would appear in the last days that would live however they wanted. He then said these people would question the promise of the return of the Lord saying that things have been continuing the same since the beginning of creation. Paul explained that the reason the Lord takes His time on this matter is because He isn't willing that any should perish (2 Pet. 3:3-9). The Bible is clear that the Lord is returning at a time when no one will expect Him. In fact, the word *expect* used in Matthew 24:44 means "to be of an opinion." This tells me that before His return there will be many opinions floating around of when He will return. But He is clear that He is going to come at a time when most will not expect. But does this mean that His coming has to be a like a thief to His people? Let me suggest to you that this does not have to be the case.

> But you, brethren, are not in darkness, so that this Day should overtake you as a thief. You are all sons of light and sons of the day. We are not of the night nor of darkness. Therefore let us not sleep, as others do, but let us watch and be sober...For God did not appoint us to wrath, but to obtain salvation through our Lord Jesus Christ (1 Thess. 5:4-6, 9).

"Overtake" means to come upon.[10] Paul is saying that the Day of the Lord shouldn't come upon us as a thief because we are sons of light and **day**. Both instances of "day" used in this passage are the same Greek word *hemera*.[11] This word speaks of the return of the Lord. Why is this significant? First, we must understand that the return of the Lord is often spoken of in the Bible as the dawning of a new day. In fact, in Malachi 4:2, Jesus is referred to as the "Sun of Righteousness." If we remain awake, watchful, and ready, His return will not be as much of a surprise as to those in darkness. Let me propose to you how this is the case.

In Genesis 18, three men visited with Abraham. One of these men was the Lord in pre-incarnate form. After prophesying to Abraham and Sarah about a future conception and birth of a son, the three headed toward Sodom. Abraham went with them for a while, which shows his desire to be in the Lord's presence. Then the Lord said, "Shall I hide from Abraham what I am doing..." (Gen. 18:17). He then shared with Abraham His assignment of investigating and possibly judging Sodom and Gomorrah for their wickedness (Gen. 18:20-22). Abraham immediately interceded for the righteous in those wicked cities (Gen. 18:23-33). The Lord promised that if there were 10 righteous in those cities, He would not destroy them. Obviously, the Lord couldn't find 10 righteous, but He did save Lot, Abraham's nephew, and part of his family. In fact, the angels literally grasped Lot and his family's hands and set them outside the city (Gen. 19:16). Genesis 19:29 tells us why the angel's went to such trouble for an obviously reluctant Lot.

> And it came to pass, when God destroyed the cities of the plain, **that God remembered Abraham,** and sent Lot out of the midst of the overthrow, when He overthrew the cities in which Lot dwelt (Gen. 19:29).

There will be two kinds of Christians at the end—those who have built an intimate, personal relationship with the Lord and those who are saved but are still closely tied to worldly affections. Those who are as Abraham will intercede for their brothers and sisters in Christ with humility and tears. And when the hour of trial comes upon the earth, He will remember those prayers and deliver those who are righteous as Lot but reluctant to let go of all they have acquired. And notice that because of Abraham's relationship with the Lord, he was in the right place at the right time to receive prophetic revelation about what God was going to do at Sodom and Gomorrah resulting in the salvation of his family. In contrast, Lot lost his home, business, family members, and more.

Coming Quickly?

> Behold, I am coming quickly! Hold fast what you have, that no one may take your crown (Rev. 3:11).

We know that God isn't a man that He should lie; yet, this scripture is puzzling. He said 2,000 years ago that He was coming quickly. So why are we are still waiting for His return? The answer is nestled in an often-overlooked Old Testament book, which might initially be just as puzzling. Even so, it is a puzzle piece we need to understand Revelation 3:11.

> Then the Lord answered me and said: "Write the vision and make it plain on tablets, that he may run who read it. For the vision is yet for an appointed time; but at the end it will speak, and it will not lie. **Though it tarries**, wait for it; because it will surely come, **it will not tarry**" (Hab. 2:2, 3).

"Though it tarries…it will not tarry." What on earth does this mean? First, we need to understand that "vision" is the Hebrew word *chazon*, which means a sight (mentally), that is, a dream, revelation, or oracle.[12] Basically, Habakkuk received a prophetic revelation in the form of a vision much like John in Revelation. And like John, God told Habakkuk to write and then declare the prophetic revelation to the people. Even so, both these visions received by these prophets were for a later time. This is what "though it tarries" means. The first "tarry" means that the vision will linger until the appointed time.[13] The next "tarry" is a different Hebrew word that means "to loiter (that is, be behind); by implication to procrastinate:—continue, defer, delay, hinder, be late (slack), stay (there), tarry (longer)."[14]

God was revealing to us a secret of prophetic revelation. First, it is important to understand that when God speaks a prophecy, He is literally birthing the future event into being. But like all babies, there is a maturing process that begins, which always involves time. Even so, the day arrives that the baby is mature. This is true of prophecy. There is an appointed day when all conditions are ripe for the prophecy to be fulfilled. When that day arrives, the prophecy will not be late. It will arrive right on time. A great example of this is in Genesis 3:15 where God prophesied that the woman's Seed would crush Satan's head (rule). This prophecy lingered for 4,000 years until conditions were perfect for Christ to come. Therefore, when Jesus said He is coming *quickly*, He was telling us that at the appointed time when all the conditions are ripe, He will return. Right now, we are in the waiting period; however, those who are wise will live each day as if He will return that day.

THE PROMISE

> He who overcomes, I will make him a pillar in the temple of My God, and he shall go out no more. I will write on him the name of My God and the name of the city of My God, the New Jerusalem, which comes down out of heaven from My God. And I will write on him My new name (Rev. 3:12).

What does it mean to be a pillar in the temple of God? In studying to answer this question, I found the story of Huram, a master craftsman, who designed the pillars of Solomon's temple, which I believe applies to the promise of being a pillar in God's temple.

> Now King Solomon sent and brought Huram from Tyre. He was the son of a widow from the tribe of Naphtali, and his father was a man of Tyre, a bronze worker; he was filled with wisdom and understanding and skill in working with all kinds of bronze work. So he came to King Solomon and did all his work. And he cast two pillars of bronze, each one eighteen cubits high, and a line of twelve cubits measured the circumference of each...Then he set up the pillars by the vestibule of the temple; he set up the pillar on the right and called its name Jachin, and he set up the pillar on the left and called its name Boaz (1 Kings 7:13-15, 21).

These two pillars were freestanding pillars meaning they didn't structurally support anything but served as symbols and reminders. *The International Standard Bible Encyclopedia* and *The Holman Bible Dictionary* states that they were probably symbolic and poetic of the pillars of heaven and earth mentioned in Job 9:6; 26:11, Psalm 75:3 and 1 Samuel 2:8. I believe they might have also stood as a reminder of the pillar of cloud and pillar of fire that the Lord used to guide the Israelites in the wilderness, which was His manifest presence in their camp. The two pillars were named Jachin and Boaz. "Jachin" means, "He shall establish"[15] and "Boaz" means, "In him is strength."[16] Clearly, the names of these pillars fit the promises Christ gave us to establish us and to strengthen us to endure until the end.

> But the Lord is faithful, **who will establish you** and guard you from the evil one (2 Thes. 3:3).
>
> Who will also confirm (also means establish) you to the end, that you may be blameless in the day of our Lord Jesus Christ (1 Cor. 1:8). *Italics mine.*
>
> Now may the God of peace Himself sanctify you completely and may your whole spirit, soul, and body be preserved blameless at the coming of our Lord Jesus Christ. He who call you is faithful, who also will do it (1 Thess. 5:23, 24).

God is establishing in His own strength a temple of God not made out of stones but out of living stones (1 Pet. 2:5). No man can boast at the end. Just as Huram was a master craftsman with bronze, Christ is a Master Craftsman of people. Jesus is fashioning us into a temple in which God Himself can dwell. The word "cast" used to describe Huram casting the pillars from bronze means fashioned.[17] In Revelation 3:12, the word "make" in the phrase, "I will make him a pillar," also means fashion.[18]

With the understanding of the significance of pillars, here is the neat part. I discovered in 2 Kings 11:14 that it was common for the king to stand by a pillar. In other words, the kings of old habitually occupied a place by a pillar. As a matter of fact, Josiah stood by one pillar and made a covenant with the Lord to restore true worship in an idolatrous nation

(2 Kings 23:3). Second Chronicles, in describing the same event, phrased it this way, "Then the king stood in his place." As pillars in His eternal temple, we will be the place where our King habitually stands, which means we will continually enjoy His presence!

On these pillars, Jesus will inscribe the name of His God, the name of the city of God, and His new name. To me, this symbolizes complete identification and possession by God, a spiritual citizenship, and a reflection of the character of Christ. In ancient times, the captives of a foreign nation were renamed according to the victorious nation's language. This occurred with Daniel and his friends (Dan. 1:7). Let us be captives of Christ. And, one final bit of information is that a city often honored a notable citizen by erecting a pillar in a temple with his name inscribed on it.

APPLICATION

Christ warned us that there will be a time when the love of many will grow cold, but he who endures to the end will be saved (Matt. 24:12, 13). The word "love" in Matthew 24:12 is *agape* love or God-love. This kind of love is only in believers (Rom. 5:5). Even in the face of persecution, the believers at Philadelphia continued in love. For this reason, they did not receive a rebuke from the Lord because "love never fails" (1 Cor. 13:8). If there is one thing I could tell you to study, live, and grow in, it is love. As this age comes to a close, we will increasingly see people we went to church with for years and friends we fellowshipped with grow cold in love and then persecute their own brothers and sisters in Christ. But if you overcome, my beloved, you will enjoy access into the very presence of the Lord on this earth and enjoy His continual presence in heaven. Therefore, stay focused on these goals of growing in love in a loveless society and enjoying His manifest presence to the fullest.

> For this reason, I bow my knees to the Father of our Lord Jesus Christ, from whom the whole family in heaven and earth is named, that He would grant you, according to the riches of His glory, to be strengthened with might through His Spirit in the inner man, that Christ may dwell in your hearts through faith; that you,

being rooted and grounded in love, may be able to comprehend with all the saints what is the width and length and depth and height—to know the love of Christ which passes knowledge; that you may be filled with all the fullness of God (Eph. 3:14-19).

Amen.

8 LAODICEA

And to the angel of the church of the Laodiceans write...
(Revelation 3:14a)

The city of Laodicea was located in southwest Asia Minor on an ancient highway that ran from Ephesus to Syria. It was close to the cities of Colossae and Hierapolis, which both had Christian communities also. In Colossians 4:12, 13, Paul mentions a man named Epaphras, whom scholars believe founded the church at Colassae. It is also believed that Paul had close contact with the churches at Laodicea and Hierapolis. Although Paul never visited Laodicea, Colossae, or Hierapolis, he held them in great affection (Col. 2:1, 4:13, 12, 16). He even wrote an epistle to the Christians at Laodicea, but it has been lost (Col. 4:16). As you will see, the Lord used all three churches in His letter to Laodicea even though only Laodicea is mentioned.

Laodicea was originally called Diospolis and then Rhoas until King Antiochus of Syria rebuilt it and named it after his wife, Laodice. Laodicea was of little importance until 190 BC when the Roman province of Asia was formed. It then became a rich, commercial city. It was so prosperous, in fact, that when an earthquake destroyed it in 60 AD along with Colossae and Hierapolis, the citizens refused financial help from Rome and rebuilt it themselves. Laodicea's wealth came from extensive banking operations and the manufacturing of its famous black wool. Laodicea also had a renowned school of medicine that had concocted a spikenard for treating ears and an eye salve.

In 1071 AD, Laodicea was taken by the Seljuks, a Turkish dynasty prominent in the 11th and 12th centuries. In 1119 AD, John Comnenus recovered Laodicea for the Christians, but it fell again to the Turks in the 13th century. Today, it is a heap of ruins called Eski Hissar, which means "old castle."

GREETING

> These things says the Amen, the Faithful and True Witness, the Beginning of the creation of God (Revelation 3:14b).

Here Jesus calls Himself three things: the Amen, the Faithful and True Witness, and the Beginning of the creation. "Amen" and "Faithful" both can mean trustworthy in the Greek.[1] "True" obviously carries the same idea, but it also means one who cannot lie.[2] "Witness" is the Greek *martus* from which we get "martyr." *Martus* means martyr, record, or witness; it also carries the idea of "one who brings to light or confirms something."[3] Jesus is the only One that can be utterly trustworthy and reliable witness of the true record of events for only He sees the hidden intents and motives of the heart. Unlike false witnesses who will lie and flatter to get what they want, the very nature of Jesus prevents Him from doing so. For this reason, He proclaimed Himself using these titles so that He could establish from the beginning that He is the only witness to their true spiritual condition, which was important because they were deceived in this area.

"Beginning" is *arche*, which means "beginning, origin, the person or thing that commences, the first person or thing in a series, the leader, that by which anything begins to be, the origin, the active cause."[4] It also means first in power or chief.[5] Interestingly, this word is used in Ephesians 6:12 for "principalities." Jesus called Satan the "prince of this world" in John 12:31. "Prince" is *archon* (root of *archon* is *arche*), which means ruler.[6] The Bible clearly states in Psalm 24:1 that the earth belongs to God. He is the Beginning and the End of all in the heavens and the earth. But if this is the case, why did Jesus call Satan the ruler of this world?

The answer lies in the fact that "world" is the Greek word *kosmos*. *Kosmos* is not used to describe the earth as far as the fact that it is a planet, but it speaks of an order or arrangement of systems and also of the inhabitants of the earth. *Kosmos* is often used to speak of the godless system that is ruled by Satan.[7]

> We know that we are of God, and that the whole world lies under the sway of the wicked one (1 Jn. 5:19).

This world system has been carefully crafted by Satan from the time that Adam handed over his authority to the serpent to the present day. He manipulates and schemes of ways to make an already godless society even worse in an attempt to defeat God and make Him a liar. However, God in His wisdom sent His Son to create an entirely new race of people who are not of this world system (1 Jn. 2:16, 17; 3:1; 4:17). These born-again believers will overcome the world system by their faith in Christ. In essence, a creative act took place again through Jesus' work on this earth. And just as God gave Adam authority to rule the earth and commanded him to multiply, Christ also gave His authority to the church and told them to multiply. The physical foreshadowed the spiritual.

Because the directives given to the church and our assignment are the same, I believe we can learn much by studying the *beginning* of the first creation. For example, why did God give Adam dominion (Gen. 1:28)? You see, "dominion" is *radah* and means to tread down, to rule, or to reign.[8] The earth was new and sin wasn't yet in the earth, so what was there to tread down? Also, God told Adam to subdue the earth. "Subdue" is *kabash* and means to tread down, conquer, keep under, and bring into subjection.[9] God gave Adam the dominion *to* subdue the earth. Here, God clearly used words that carry the idea of war, military, and conquering. But why did a perfect, sinless earth need to be conquered?

> Then the Lord God took the man and put him in the garden of Eden to tend and keep it (Gen. 2:15).

"Keep" is *shamar* and means to watch or to guard.[10] It can also mean watchman. Watchmen were those who walked the walls of a city to watch for any people approaching. A good watchman could discern if the individuals approaching were friends or foes at great distances. They then relayed the information to the king who ordered the gates of the city closed or opened based on the watchman's observances. As you can see, God used a word that means more than pruning trees in the garden. He was telling Adam to actively watch for and guard against any enemy for he knew that Satan was prowling about looking for some way to rule since he lost his exalted position in heaven. Adam and Eve were immediate targets of Satan for they were God's beloved creation, and Satan knew that God had given the earth into their hands (Ps. 115:16). To cause them to obey him over God meant that he could exact revenge for God casting him out of His presence and destroy mankind's destiny by stealing it.

The Bible tells us that God is faithful even when we are not (2 Tim. 2:13) and that He never goes back on His word (Rom. 11:29); therefore, when man gave dominion of the earth to the enemy, the earth was transferred to Satan's rule. That is why Satan could offer Jesus the kingdoms of the earth if only He worshiped him (Matt. 4:9). Even so, God had a plan from the beginning. He told Satan that the woman's Seed would crush his head (authority). God sent His Son in the form of man for only man could win back what was lost. You see, man was given authority, and man gave that authority away. Only a man could get it back, but it couldn't be just any man for all men born after the fall were in the image of fallen man (Gen. 5:3). For this reason, Jesus was created as 100% man and 100% God; the first in a race of new creatures. Jesus stripped Satan of his authority by remaining sinless and overcoming death. He has now given that authority to all who believe in Him (Lk. 10:19). Now the same commission that was given to Adam is given to us: we have dominion and we are to subdue. However, we, too, must watch for serpents in our gardens—places in which we have authority—such as our homes, marriages, families, and jobs.

EXORTATION

> I know your works, that you are neither cold nor hot. I could wish you were cold or hot. So then, because you are lukewarm, and neither cold nor hot, I will vomit you out of My mouth (Revelation 3:15, 16).

Jesus begins His discourse the same as He did the other churches by saying, "I know your works." However, Laodicea is the only church of the seven that did not receive a commendation from the Lord, which is astonishing because it means that there was nothing good in this church to commend. Jesus loved this church enough to confront its condition in order to restore. Also, the greatest promise given to any of the churches was given to this church.

Hot Or Cold

In referring to this church's works, Jesus said that they were neither hot nor cold and then He voices His desire that He wished they were one or the other. Many have taught that Jesus desires us to be on fire for Him or completely cold to Him. But this doesn't make sense, so I dug a little bit and discovered some interesting facts.

First, it's important to remember that the Bible was written to real people in real places with real concerns. Often what is written in the Bible has an immediate application to those it was first written to and a prophetic application for those who would come later. Second, it is also important to understand that Jesus' teaching style included using people, places, and nature to make His points. He repeatedly did this in the parables, so it makes sense that He would use the same teaching style in these letters. Before we examine how He did this in this letter, let's examine the Greek of hot and cold. In the Greek, "hot" means to be fervent or zealous for God.[11] "Cold" literally means chilly, but it comes from the Greek word, *psuch,* that means to breath, blow.[12] Read the following scripture.

> And they heard the sound of the Lord God walking in
> the garden in the cool of the day, and Adam and his wife
> hid themselves from the presence of the Lord God
> among the trees of the garden (Gen 3:8).

"Sound" literally means voice,[13] and "cool" literally means wind or breeze.[14] The beginning of Genesis 3:8 could read, "And they heard the voice of the Lord God walking in the garden in the breeze of the day." How beautiful! Can you picture Adam and Eve listening to His voice on the breeze? It denotes intimacy because a breeze is gentle. The

Holy Spirit's voice is also gentle (1 Kings 19:12). In essence, Jesus was saying, "I want you fervent for Me or intimate with Me." Of course, we can see that both of these would denote a close relationship with Him, which is why He said He desired that they were either hot or cold.

As stated above, Jesus had something in mind when He told Laodicea they were neither cold nor hot, and the church there would have known exactly what He meant. Remember that Laodicea was close to two cities, Colassae and Hierapolis. All three cities had Christian communities within them and knew of each other. When Jesus said that He wished they were cold, He was bringing up the fact that the city of Colassae had cold, pure waters that people could refresh themselves with. When He said that He wished they were hot, He was referring to the therapeutic hot springs located in Hierapolis. Both these waters were beneficial to their users. In contrast, Laodicea didn't have its own water source. Instead, they had built a five- to six-mile-long aqueduct that supplied its citizens with tepid or lukewarm water. According to *Zodhiates,* lukewarm water isn't good for anything other than an emetic (induces vomiting). You can see that Jesus was telling this church that they didn't have cold refreshing waters for the spiritually weary and thirsty to drink, and they didn't have hot, therapeutic waters for the spiritually sick.

Deception

> Because you say, "I am rich, have become wealthy, and have need of nothing"—and do not know that you are wretched, miserable, poor, blind, and naked—I counsel you to buy from Me gold refined in the fire, that you may be rich; and white garments, that you may be clothed, that the shame of your nakedness may not be revealed; and anoint your eyes with eye salve, that you may see (Rev. 3:17, 18).

Remember that Laodicea was a very wealthy city, which meant some of that wealth went to the church there. The Laodiceans thought that the material wealth they enjoyed was a sign of God's approval as many Christians do today in prosperous societies; yet, Jesus reveals that they are wretched, miserable, poor, blind and naked! Jesus' disciples learned this truth when the rich young ruler came to Him asking how to obtain eternal life.

> Now behold, one came and said to Him, "Good Teacher, what good thing shall I do that I may obtain eternal life? So He said to Him, "Why do you call Me good? No one is good but One, that is, God. But if you want to enter into life, keep the commandments." He said to Him, "Which ones?" Jesus said, "You shall not murder." "You shall not commit adultery." "You shall not steal." "You shall not bear false witness." "Honor your father and your mother." "You shall love your neighbor as yourself." The young man said to Him, "All these things I have kept from my youth. What do I still lack?" Jesus said to him, "If you want to be perfect, go, sell what you have and give to the poor, and you will have treasure in heaven; and come, follow Me." But when the young man heard that saying, he went away sorrowful, for he had great possessions (Mt. 19:16-22).

This young man was not a casual seeker for from an early age, he had kept all the commandments listed. But notice that these commandments only dealt with his relationship with man not with God. Amazingly, this young ruler had sense enough to know that something was still missing, but he didn't know what. Jesus immediately went to the heart of the issue by exposing the idolatry in his heart concerning wealth, which prevented an intimate relationship with God for you cannot serve two masters (Mt. 6:24). Sadly, the young ruler went away unwilling to give up his wealth.

Jesus then explained to His disciples that it is easier for a camel to go through the eye of a needle than a rich man to enter the kingdom of God, which astonished His disciples for they believed as many today that wealth was a sign of God's approval (Mt. 19:23-25). Again, Jesus used an illustration to make His point. In ancient times, entrances to houses, some city gates, and other buildings were low and narrow and were often called needle-eyes. In order for a camel to enter one of these entrances, the animal had to kneel down, have his load removed, and shuffle through the gate on his knees. Jesus was revealing that while prosperity in itself is not evil, most people do not handle it correctly for they become prideful in their wealth. Entering the kingdom of God demands humility.

I fear that much of the American church believes as the Laodicean church did. Compared to other countries with the exception of maybe Western Europe, Americans have an abundance of teaching, worship music, churches, Bible translations, Bible colleges, Christian television, etc.; yet we are spiritually poor, wretched, miserable, blind, and naked. Could this be why the demonstration of the power of God is so missing in America? Are we so filled with all that our society has to offer that we do not hunger and thirst after righteousness? Is it that we are so blind to our true condition that we don't recognize our need for something more than weekly church services and an occasional book? The true riches are spiritual in nature, but we won't be trusted with these if we can't properly handle unrighteous money.

I want to point out something that I believe God revealed to me about America and the enemy's plan to destroy her. First, I want to state emphatically that I believe America is one of the best countries on the planet. We always run to the help of others when disasters strike. We give more money away than any other nation. We have more freedoms than most nations, and we have amazing people who live here. But we also have some serious things wrong with us. Read Ezekiel 16:49-50:

> Look, this is the iniquity of your sister Sodom: She and her daughter had pride, fullness of food, and abundance of idleness; neither did she strengthen the hand of the poor and needy. And they were haughty and committed abomination before Me; therefore I took them away as I saw fit.

Many believe that Sodom and Gomorrah were destroyed because of rampant homosexuality, and that was a contributing factor. But Ezekiel reveals that it was also pride, fullness of food, too much idle time, and not helping the poor. The homosexuality was the icing on the cake. I believe that we are a country that helps the poor, but if you examine many of those who attend church and call themselves Christians, they are very reluctant to give even their tithe. For many, it is fear or a lack of understanding the purpose of tithing. Still others don't want to let go of that ten percent. We would do well to realize that tithing isn't only a personal issue that must be resolved. Tithing is a corporate issue that affects the church as a whole. In Malachi's famous passage concerning tithing, God addressed the entire nation of Israel (Mal. 3:9). What would happen if every Christian tithed? We would enter a season of divine favor and blessing that no devil in hell could stop, and we would be able to further God's kingdom in ways only dreamed about.

Am I saying America and the church in America is going to be judged? All nations will be judged after the church is judged (1 Pet. 4:17). But our judgment will be determined by the condition we are in at that time. I believe God showed me that the enemy sees some of the same things in America that were in Sodom and Gomorrah; therefore, he knows that if he can get homosexuality legalized and accepted as a "normal" lifestyle, then God must judge. As a church, we need to wake up to this truth, pray, and give. Don't be deceived into thinking that God approves of you, your church, and this country because we are prosperous. Instead, ask yourself if you are using your prosperity to further His kingdom and do you have true riches?

True Riches

> I counsel you to buy from Me gold refined in the fire, that you may be rich; and white garments, that you may be clothed, that the shame of your nakedness may not be revealed; and anoint your eyes with eye salve, that you may see (Rev. 3:18).

When the all-knowing, all-wise Lord gives counsel, the wise listen and do what He says (Prov. 1:5). "Counsel" in this verse simply means to give advice or recommend.[15] In *Webster's New World Dictionary advice* is an "opinion given as to what to do or how to handle a situation." Jesus has already stated their situation as the True Witness. Now He is telling them what to do to fix it. God never tears down without building up. Even in bringing His judgments, He always gives hope to the one being judged. In fact, His judgments are motivated by love—love for the person who needs discipline and love for those the person might be hurting. Also, His judgments are designed to remove anything that offends love. His judgments are righteous and true balanced by mercy and truth (Ps. 89:14). Jesus advised the church at Laodicea to buy three things: refined gold, white garments, eye salve.

Refined Gold, White Garments, and Eye Salve

Gold is mentioned more than any other metal in the Bible (approximately 394 times) and is symbolic of things of great value. However, gold in its raw and impure state is not pliable; therefore, it must be refined by fire. This is a time-consuming and difficult process because the temperature of the fire must be perfect in order to draw the impurities to the surface. Once the impurities rise to the surface, the refiner ladles them off, and the process starts again. The refiner knows the refining process is complete when he can see his reflection in the gold.

The refined gold Jesus recommended can only be bought from Him because we can't purify ourselves; instead, we must allow His refining process in our lives to remove all impurities from our hearts. The fire that the great Refiner uses is trials, tests, and tribulations. He knows the perfect temperature to keep the fire so that the refining process is not hindered. This can be a difficult process because as the impurities in a person's heart surfaces, the individual begins to wonder what is wrong with him. You see, when being purified, wrong thoughts, wrong emotions, wrong actions often come out. For example, if you think you are a patient person, you will find during a refining process that you aren't as patient as you thought you were. Even so, these impurities have risen to the top so that they are exposed and the Refiner can ladle them off. As we allow the refining process to continue, our hearts become more soft and pliable. Soon, the Refiner sees His reflection in the gold. It is in this state that we are resistant to rust and corruption, and we are transparent (Rev. 21:21).

Remember that earlier we learned that Jesus teaches by using things around us as examples? He does here also. When Jesus counseled these believers to buy from Him refined gold, He had in mind Laodicea's extensive banking operations that produced great wealth. Jesus was refocusing this body of believers by pointing them to a refined life that is more valuable than all the gold in the world.

> He will sit as a refiner and a purifier of silver; He will purify the sons of Levi, and purge them as gold and silver, that they may offer to the Lord an offering of righteousness (Mal. 3:3).

The second item Jesus counseled them to buy was white garments. In Scripture, garments represent how we live—righteously or unrighteously. The church at Laodicea would instantly think of the fact that their city was famous for its black wool. Again Jesus was using the characteristics of their city as object lessons for them. It is also important to understand that black often represents darkness while white represents righteousness.

> Let us be glad and rejoice and give Him glory, for the marriage of the Lamb has come, and His wife has made herself ready. And to her it was granted to be arrayed in fine linen, clean and bright, **for the fine linen is the righteous acts of the saints** (Rev. 19:7, 8).

> I will greatly rejoice in the Lord, my soul shall be joyful in my God; **for He has clothed me with the garments of salvation, He has covered me with the robe of righteousness**, as a bridegroom decks himself with ornaments, and as a bride adorns herself with her jewels (Isa. 61:10).

The imagery in the above scriptures is of a wedding. In Isaiah 61:10, the Lord provided the clothing of salvation and righteousness. In Revelation 19:7, 8, the bride made herself ready. These scriptures illustrate the fact that Jesus, through His death, burial, and resurrection, provided us with righteousness, but that is only the beginning. We must also put on righteousness by living according to His Word. Many see the initial salvation experience as the beginning and the end not realizing that we are to work out our salvation with fear and trembling (Phil. 2:12). Salvation is an inception and a process. We can refuse to wear His garments of salvation and righteousness even after we accept Him as our Savior by practicing disobedience. James made it clear that our faith must be mixed with corresponding works of righteousness (Jms. 2:22).

> Awake, awake! Put on your strength, O Zion; put on your beautiful garments, O Jerusalem, the holy city! For the uncircumcised and the unclean shall no longer come to you (Isa. 52:1).

> But put on the Lord Jesus Christ and make no provision for the flesh, to fulfill its lusts (Rom. 13:14).

> That you put off, concerning our former conduct, the old man which grows corrupt according to the deceitful lusts, and be renewed in the spirit of your mind, and that you put on the new man which was created according to God, in true righteousness and holiness (Eph. 4:22-24).

Human nature is one of extremes. It is rare to find anyone, even one who is a Christian, who is balanced. For example, throughout the centuries God has repeatedly restored truths that were lost. One that might be the best example is Martin Luther's truth that we are saved by faith. During his lifetime, people could purchase sin and purchase forgiveness. But Martin Luther discovered in the Bible that this was not scriptural, so he nailed his 95 theses supporting the truths he learned to a church door at Wittenberg. This sparked a major shift in the church resulting in the Reformation.

Another truth that God restored to the church was holiness, which actually was birthed during Martin Luther's time. It is called the "Holiness Movement" and birthed the Pentecostal movement. This truth states that a Christian should live a holy life through the power of the Holy Spirit. But what happened is that the church went into a ditch that resulted in legalism—a set of rules that Christians must live by in order to be deemed as holy. Various rules included: men can't have long hair, women must have long hair, and women cannot wear makeup or pants, and more. If you didn't follow these rules, you were not a true Christian. Also, love was not often preached among holiness preachers. Many messages about hell, God's judgment, and fear of the Lord were preached.

To fix this problem, God began to restore the truth of His love toward His people and sinners. But like we have done with most of the truths He restored, we have swung over to the other ditch. Now many believe that love covers any lifestyle and sin. We have Christians who refuse to confront other Christians in serious sin. When a Christian hurts his brother or sister in Christ, the one hurt is encouraged to simply forgive and let it go. The clear Biblical mandate of the Lord in Matthew 18 is not carried out. Of course, some people are easily offended and petty. But there are legitimate issues that must be dealt with correctly that are not. Fear of the Lord has been replaced with a mindset that God's grace and love will forgive anything. This out-of-balance love doctrine has resulted in lawlessness in the church and an inability to recognize predators.

> For certain men have crept in unnoticed, who long ago were marked out for this condemnation, ungodly men, who turn the grace of our God into lewdness (unbridled lust) and deny the only Lord God and our Lord Jesus Christ (Jude 4).

Later Jude instructed us to make a distinction. He said to have compassion and mercy but also to have fear so that when we are helping a brother who has fallen, we should hate "the garment defiled by the flesh" (Jude 22-23). In other words, we need to recognize the predators and not allow them to seduce the sheep. But we should also recognize those who are in serious sin that want help. If that is the case, we are to help them but with fear of the Lord, which means we will hate the sin and be careful not to be tainted by it.

The Bible is clear that there are garments of salvation and righteousness, garments of legalism, and garments of lawlessness. As we learned earlier, the parable of the wedding feast in Matthew 22:1-14 illustrates this truth and is worth repeating. In this parable the king arranges a marriage for his son. He sends out his servants to those who were previously invited to the wedding, but they refuse to come. Some even seize the king's servants and killed them. The king was furious, and he sent his armies to destroy their city by fire.

He then sends servants into the highways to invite as many as they can. They obeyed and the wedding hall was filled with guests. But when the king came in to see the guests, he notices one man who did not have on a wedding garment. It is important to understand the culture of Jesus' time. Whenever a father, especially one of wealth, held a wedding supper for his son and his bride, he provided wedding garments for those who didn't have any or those who had traveled a great distance to be at the supper and hadn't had a chance to purchase appropriate garments. Typically, the garments were white robes. To refuse to wear a wedding garment was considered a grievous insult to the father and the wedding party. In fact, the person who refused was often asked to leave and in some cases, the offender was punished.

In this parable, the king represents the Father, and the son is Jesus Christ. The marriage is to His bride, which is the church made up of both Jew and Gentile believers. Before the Father invited the Gentiles, He sent His servants, the prophets, to Israel to invite them to the wedding. But Israel killed her prophets and refused to come. In other words, they rejected the Messiah in favor of religion. In 70 A.D., the Roman armies besieged Jerusalem and burned the temple and city to the ground.

The Father then sent His servants to the highways, which represents other nations or the Gentiles. These accepted the invitation to His wedding, so the Father provided them wedding garments, which represent their righteous acts (Rev. 19:8). All but one puts these garments on. I believe that this man who refused to put on the wedding garments thought his garments were fine for the wedding, which can represent religious works (legalism) or sinful works (lawlessness) as we discussed above. When confronted, this guest was speechless and was removed from the wedding hall. The phrase in verse 13, "Cast him into outer darkness; there will be weeping and gnashing of teeth" is a phrase used by the religious leaders when excommunicating a Jew from their synagogue. The implication is that this person was excommunicated from the presence of God and His people.

> But we are all like an unclean thing, and **all our righteousness are like filthy rags** (lit. a filthy garment);

> we all fade as a leaf, and our iniquities, like the wind, have taken us away (Isa. 64:6).

> And be found in Him, **not having my own righteousness, which is from the law,** but that which is through faith in Christ, the righteousness which is from God by faith (Phil. 3:9).

> Now the works of the flesh are evident, which are: adultery,[a] fornication, uncleanness, lewdness, idolatry, sorcery, hatred, contentions, jealousies, outbursts of wrath, selfish ambitions, dissensions, heresies, envy, murders, drunkenness, revelries, and the like; of which I tell you beforehand, just as I also told *you* in time past, that those who practice such things will not inherit the kingdom of God (Gal. 5:19-21).

> Blessed *are* those who do His commandments, that they may have the right to the tree of life, and may enter through the gates into the city. But outside *are* dogs and sorcerers and sexually immoral and murderers and idolaters, and whoever loves and practices a lie (Rev. 22:14, 15).

The third and final item He counseled them to buy was eye salve so that they could see. Again, Jesus had in His mind the fact that Laodicea had a renowned medical school famous for the eye salve it concocted. This body of believers was blind to the Truth. Only Jesus' eye salve could open the eyes of their hearts to revelation knowledge of Him and their condition.

Love Rebukes

> As many as I love, I rebuke and chasten. Therefore be zealous and repent (Rev. 3:19).

Even though this church did not receive a commendation, Jesus softened His rebuke by letting them know that He loves them and out of that love, He must rebuke and discipline. "Rebuke" means to convince or tell a fault.[16] He couldn't let this church continue as it was because it would have ruined them. He had to expose their sin so they could gain understanding and repent.

> He who spares his rod hates his son, but he who loves him disciplines him promptly (Prov. 13:240.

> And have you forgotten the exhortation which speaks to you as to sons: "My son, do not despise the chastening of the Lord, nor be discouraged when you are rebuked by Him; for whom the Lord loves He chastens, and scourges every son whom He receives." If you endure chastening, God deals with you as with sons; for what son is there whom a father does not chasten? But if you are without chastening, of which all have become partakers, then you are illegitimate and not sons (Heb. 12:5-8).

Sadly, many in the body of Christ today do not understand the necessity of confronting others that are sinning or deceived. Many Christians separate love from justice believing that discipline is a last resort when love fails. But God's love, justice, and righteousness are intertwined and cannot be separated. Love always confronts for Love is a Person who is also Truth.

> Behold, I stand at the door and knock. If anyone hears My voice and opens the door, I will come in to him and dine with him, and he with Me (Rev. 3:20).

This verse has been hard for me to understand. It's almost like a paradox. Why is Jesus standing outside and knocking? He's the Lord! He should be granted entrance day and night into His church without knocking. That He is outside of this church shows their condition and blindness. Remember that they thought they were fine. In fact, they probably thought that God was in their church. What a surprise to find He was outside knocking to get in His own church!

This scripture reveals the balance between God's grace and personal responsibility. It is His grace that He knocks and calls to His sheep to open the door. He could just write off lukewarm believers and give His attention to those that are on fire for Him. But He doesn't. He leaves the 99 and goes after the one (Mt. 18:10-14). Even so, each of us has the personal responsibility to hear His voice and open the door when He comes. Here, opening the door requires zealous repentance of their lukewarm condition (Rev. 3:19). The result is restored intimacy, which is represented by His desire to dine with them. Dining in the Middle Eastern culture is always associated with intimacy.

> Let your waist be girded and your lamps burning; and you yourselves be like men who wait for their master, when he will return from the wedding, **that when he comes and knocks they may open to him immediately**. Blessed are those servants whom the master, when he comes, will find watching. Assuredly, I say to you that he will gird himself and have them sit down to eat, and will come serve them…Therefore you also be ready, for the Son of Man is coming at an hour you do not expect…Blessed is that servant whom his master will find so doing when he comes. Truly, I say to you that he will make him ruler over all that he has (Lk. 12:35-37, 40, 43-48).

THE PROMISE

> To him who overcomes I will grant to sit with Me on My throne, as I also overcame and sat down with My Father on His throne (Rev. 3:21).

Of all the churches, He promises the greatest promise to the one least deserving. It reminds me of the parable of the vineyard workers. In this parable, Jesus tells of a landowner who hired laborers for his vineyard. The first he hired at 6 a.m. were guaranteed a denarius a day. He then hired more laborers at the third hour, the sixth hour, the ninth hour, and the eleventh hour promising those just wages.

> So when evening had come, the owner of the vineyard said to his steward, "Call the laborers and give them their wages, beginning with the last to the first." And

when those who came who were hired at the eleventh hour, they each received a denarius. But when the first came, they supposed that they would receive more; and they likewise received each a denarius. And when they received it, they complained against the landowner, saying, "These last men have worked only one hour, and you made them equal to us who have borne the burden and the heat of the day." But he answered one of them and said, "Friend, I am doing you no wrong. Did you not agree with me for a denarius? Take what is yours and go your way, I wish to give this last man the same as you… So the **last will be first, and the first last.** For many are called, but few chosen (Matt. 20:8-14, 16).

I'm sure you can see the prophetic in this parable. The last body of believers alive at His return will receive the same reward as those who lived 2,000 years ago. Many Christian teachers say that the church at Laodicea represents the last-day church. We represent the laborer hired at the eleventh hour. And if we overcome epidemic lukewarmness, we will receive the same reward as other believers in previous ages and an even greater promise of sitting on His throne. I believe this is because lukewarmness is one of the most difficult things to overcome.

As you can see, the Laodicean church can go either way. Their decision will produce judgment or incredible blessing, which brings me to the meaning of Laodicea. Laodicea is two Greek words: *laos* and *dike*. *Laos* means a people, nation, or a number of people joined together by the common bonds of society.[17] *Dike* basically means the assertion by human society of a certain standard expected by its people which, if not kept, can bring forth ensuing judgment.[18] *Dike* occurs only four times in the Bible and is translated in the NKJV as judgment, justice, destruction, and vengeance (Acts 25:15, 28:4; 2 Thess. 1:9; Jude 1:7). We, as a church, are a kingdom, a people, a nation of kings and priests (*laos*). Jesus has set a standard of righteousness for us that we can keep because the Spirit of God dwells within us and empowers us (*dike*). Even so, the choice is ours and will result in a judgment for or against us.

> For if God did not spare the natural branches, He may not spare you either. Therefore, consider the goodness and severity of God: on those who fell, severity; but toward you, goodness, IF you continue in His goodness. Otherwise you also will be cut off (Rom. 11:21, 22).

Jesus always comes as a Lamb first, but if He is rejected as a Lamb, He will then come as the Lion.

APPLICATION

> He who has an ear, let him hear what the Spirit says to the churches (Rev. 3:22).

As believers, we must beware of self-sufficiency that leads to complacency and a false sense of security especially in a prosperous society. We must also be watchful and guard the garden God has given us—our families, jobs, spiritual life, ministry—from the crafty serpent. Jesus told us to be as wise as the serpent (Mt. 10:16). We must not be ignorant of the way the enemy works and his schemes. He will attempt to deceive us through thoughts, other people, circumstances, false teachings, and spiritual predators.

What garments are you wearing? Are you in the ditch of legalism or lawlessness? Do you submit to God's chastisement and refining? We should not waste our trials for they are meant to work in us the character of Christ. Don't be deceived into thinking that God approves of you because you are prospering or your ministry is prospering. The true test of faith is obedience to Him and His Word.

Those who teach and preach the Word must provide messages that stir up the faith of the people instead of lulling them to sleep. Are they messages that tickle the ears comforting the flesh or messages that challenge them to come up higher in their spiritual walk? It is important to realize that all Christians, but especially leaders, must confront sin in other Christians. This might be done through messages, but it should also be done one on one. Obviously, a pastor must confront serious sin in his congregation for the benefit of the one sinning and those who could be hurt in his flock. As individuals, we can pray for a strategy and the words to say to those who are our friends or family members that are sinning. It has been my experience that 90% of the time, this type of loving confrontation produces good results.

We have been living in the last days since Jesus came, and these days are dangerous (2 Tim. 3:1-5). Even so, the Lord promised that as the days grew darker, we would become brighter (Isa. 60:1, 2). Daniel prophesied that during these times those that know their God will do mighty exploits (Dan. 11:32). And that is the key: knowing God. Intimacy with Christ is the key to surviving the times we are in. We must be aggressive in having regular intimate time with Him for this is eternal life here on earth and later in heaven (Jn. 17:3).

BIBLIOGRAPHY

Chapter 1: Intro

[1]James Strong, *The New Strong's Exhaustive Concordance of the Bible*, (Nashville: Thomas Nelson Publishers, 1984) ref. no. G602

[2]Ibid., G5604

[3]Ibid, G32

[4]Ibid, G2033

[5]Spiros Zodhiates, *The Complete Word Study Dictionary: New Testament* (Chattanooga, TN, 1992) ref. no. G2033

[6]Roman Road Bible Studies. 2009. <http://www.romansroad.org/bible-studies/article/index.php?page=9>.

Chapter 2: Ephesus

[1]Strong's G2902

[2]Parson's Quickverse Software, version 7.0 (Cedar Rapids, IA, Parson's Technology Inc, 2000): *Thayer's Greek Definitions* (Institute for Creation Research, El Cajon, CA, 1999).

[3]Strong's, G4043

[4]Ibid, G652

[5]Ibid, G652

[6]Ibid, G3345

[7]Ibid, G3339

[8]Zodhiates, ref. No 3345

[9]Strong's, G5281

[10]Thayer's, G863

[11]Ibid, G3421

[12]Zodiates, ref. no. 1601

[13]Ibid, G3340

[14]Ibid, G5545

[15]Strong's, G5530

[16]Strong's, G3857; Thayer's, G3857

Chapter 3: Smyrna

[1]Strong's G4668

[2]Ibid, G1492

[3]Ibid, G4432

[4]Zodhiates, ref. no. 4432

[5]Strong's, H376

[6]Ibid, H120

[7]Ibid, H7069

[8]Ibid, H7014

[9]Ibid, H7779

[10]Ibid, H7218

[11]Ibid, H8159

[12]Ibid, H3120

[13]Ibid, G3196

[14] 2010, Dictionary.com LLC, <http://dictionary.reference.com/browse/ferment>

[15] Strong's, G2219

[16] Ibid, G5399

[17] Ibid, G4735

Chapter 4: Pergamos

[1] Strong's G4010

[2] Rick Joynor, *A Prophetic History: Part One,* (Fort Mill, SC: MorningStar Publications, 2009)

[3] Zodhiates, ref. no. 2087; Strong's, G2087

[4] Ibid, ref. no. 243

[5] Strong's, G2098

[6] Zodhiates, ref. no. 4625

[7] Strong's, H1109

[8] Ibid, G4487

[9] Ibid, G3056

[10] Ibid, 3433

[11] Ibid, G765

[12] Zodiates, ref. no. 2537

[13] Ibid, ref. no. 3686

[14] Strong's, H3290

[15] Ibid, H3478

Chapter 5: Thyatira

[1] Zodhiates, ref. no. 2363

[2] Strong's, G5474

[3] Ibid, G1439

[4] Ibid, G1135

[5] Zodhiates, ref. no. 5550

[6] Thayer's, G3340

[7] Strong's, G3173 and G2347

[8] Thayer's, G5043

[9] Ibid, G1849

[10] <u>Spirit-Filled Life Bible; New King James Version</u> (Thomas Nelson, Nashville, TN. 1991). Word Wealth at 1 Corinthians 15:23

[11] Strong's, G3101

[12] Note I said the fall of mankind. Scripture is clear that from the fall to the second coming, 6000 years will pass. We don't know how long Adam and Eve lived on the earth before the fall. We do know that it was long enough to begin populating the earth, because when Cain left as a vagabond, he went to the land of Nod, which was already populated (Gen. 4:16-24).

Chapter 6: Sardis

[1] Thayer's, G3686

[2] Strong's, G4790

[3] Ibid, G1127

[4] Ibid, 3435

⁵Parson's Quickverse Software, version 7.0 (Cedar Rapids, IA, Parson's Technology Inc, 2000): *Barnes Notes on the Old Testament*

Chapter 7: Philadelphia

¹Parson's Quickverse Software, version 7.0 (Cedar Rapids, IA, Parson's Technology Inc, 2000): James Orr, *International Bible Encyclopedia*

²Strong's, G5359

³Ibid, H7644

⁴Ibid. H471

⁵Ibid, H776

⁶Zodhiates, ref. no. 575

⁷Ibid, ref. no. 1537

⁸Strong's, G5083

⁹Ibid, G5610

¹⁰Ibid, G2638

¹¹Ibid, G2250

¹²Ibid, H2377

¹³Ibid, H4102

¹⁴Ibid, H309

¹⁵Ibid, H3199

¹⁶Ibid, H1162

¹⁷Ibid, H6696

¹⁸Thayer's, G4160

Chapter 8: Laodicea

[1] Strong's, G281; Ibid, G4103

[2] Zodhiates, ref. no. 228

[3] Strong's, G3144; Zodhiates, ref. no. 3144

[4] zodhiates, ref. no. 746

[5] Strong's, G746

[6] Ibid, G758

[7] Ibid, G2889; Zodhiates, ref. no. 2889

[8] Strong's, H7287

[9] Ibid, H3533

[10] Ibid, H8104

[11] Zodhiates, ref. no. 2200

[12] Ibid, ref. no. 5593

[13] Strong's, H6963

[14] Ibid, H7307

[15] Ibid, G4823

[16] Ibid, G1651

[17] Ibid, G2992

[18] Zodhiates, ref. no. 1349

ABOUT THE AUTHOR

Sherri Wilson and her husband, Mike Wilson, founded Free Indeed and Power September, 2007 and later, The Furnace, a weekly gathering focused solely on worship and restoration of true New Testament Christianity, along with Cory Lucero, the worship leader, June 2012. They are committed to seeing the Kingdom on earth manifesting God's dominion through worship, the Word, and signs and wonders confirming. She is committed to seeing the saints equipped and trained for ministry based out of intimacy with God—working with Him not for Him.

She has been in the marketplace with several businesses for 15 years and has learned many life lessons from Holy Spirit there. She takes not just the spiritual lessons but also the knowledge she has gained as a pioneer and builder of businesses into ministry and takes joy in her part of rebuilding the Tabernacle of David.

Sherri and her husband live in New Mexico and have one son who is the lead musician of The Furnace Band.

For more information, please contact:

Free Indeed and Power

917 E 10th

Clovis, NM 88101

www.freeinpower.com

Most of our teachings including from conferences are online free for download or listening. Also, have articles, Bible studies, videos, and more!